The Book

Exploring, Understanding and Embracing the Buffet of God's Blessings through the Symbolism of the Table

Jermaine E. Pennington

L.E.A.D. Publishing Group Copyright @ 2025

ALL RIGHTS RESERVED. No portion of this publication may be reproduced, stored in any electronic system, or transmitted in any form or by any means, electronic, mechanical, photocopy, recording or otherwise, without the written permissions from the author and publisher. Brief quotations may be used in literary Reviews.

All Scriptures used in this text are from the New Revised Standard Version (NIV). Any other translation used herein will be clearly indicated within the text. Copyright© by Thomas Nelson, Inc. Used by permission. All rights reserved.

ISBN: 9798339687184

Table of Content

Introduction: "The Significance and Meaning of the Table"
Page 6

Chapter 1: The Covenant
Page 13

Chapter 2: The Table is Spread
Page 38

Chapter 3: Saying Grace
Page 75

Chapter 4: Table Manners
Page 100

Chapter 5: Guess Who's Coming to Dinner
Page 139

Chapter 6: The Coming Feast
Page 179

Notes:
Page 208

Dedication:

To those who have felt invisible, overlooked, and unworthy of a seat at the "cool table"—know this: God sees you, knows you, and lovingly invites you to sit at His table, where there is always a place reserved just for you.

To those who are anxious about where their next provision will come from—at God's table, He will provide abundantly, filling every need and quenching every thirst with the riches of His love and faithfulness.

To those who are wrestling with understanding the depth and breadth of God's radical grace—at His table, you will encounter the most life-altering lesson yet to be revealed, a grace that transcends all human understanding and heals every wounded heart.

This book is dedicated to you—your longing, your hunger, and your relentless pursuit of a bread that this earth cannot provide. May you find in these pages an invitation to dine at the table of the Divine, where there is fullness of joy, an endless supply of grace, and a feast of love that will satisfy your soul forever.

Introduction: "The Significance and Meaning of the Table"

In every culture, the table is far more than just a place to eat; it's a stage where the drama of life unfolds. The table is where we gather to share meals, tell stories, and forge connections with others. This humble piece of furniture takes on a starring role in our lives, symbolizing community, culture, and covenant. As I sit at the well-worn oak table in my dining room, I'm overwhelmed with a flood of family memories—of laughter, tears, celebrations, and even tough conversations. It's remarkable to consider the historical and cultural significance of the table and how it serves as a bridge connecting us to the grand, ongoing story of humanity and the divine.

The table is central to human experience. Across every culture, from grand banquets to simple family dinners, the table serves as a place of gathering. It's where families come together at the end of the day to share their stories, where friends meet to catch up over a meal, and where communities celebrate life's milestones and holidays. In my family tradition, the table is more than just a place to eat—it's where the real action happens. It's where Spades and Dominos are slapped down with earth-shaking force, each thundering smack not just a declaration of competitive dominance but a powerful affirmation of our togetherness.

But it's not just about whose winning; every loud, triumphant slam of a card or tile is also a way of saying, *"We're here together, and that's what really matters."* The table isn't just where we eat; it's where we bond, where laughter reverberates through the room, and where the strength of our unity is felt with every well-placed move.

The table is a place of nourishment—not just for the body, but for the soul. Around the table, we find comfort, belonging, and connection. It's a space where memories are made, where traditions are passed down, and where the essence of family and friendship is celebrated. The table, in its many forms, is where life's most meaningful moments unfold, reminding us that, at its core, it's not just about the food on our plates, but the people seated around it.

Culturally, the table is a powerful symbol. It represents the heart of the home, the place where traditions are passed down from one generation to the next. Whether it's the Thanksgiving dinner table in America, the communal dining practices in many Asian cultures, or the elaborate feasts of the Mediterranean, the table is where cultural identity is both expressed and preserved. The rituals surrounding the table—how food is prepared, served, and shared—are deeply ingrained in our cultural consciousness. They tell the story of who we are, where we come from, and what we value.

But the significance of the table goes even deeper. It is a symbol of covenant. In many religious traditions, the table is a sacred space where the divine meets the human. In Christianity, for example, the table is where the Lord's Supper, or Communion, is celebrated—a ritual that commemorates the covenant between God and humanity through the sacrifice of Jesus Christ. This act of breaking bread and sharing wine is not just a remembrance of a past event, but a participation in an ongoing, living covenant that transcends time and space. It's a powerful reminder that the table is not just a place of physical nourishment, but also a place of spiritual sustenance, where God's presence is made real in our lives.

My family's table stands as a silent witness to the unfolding story of my life and that of my family. It's where we've celebrated birthdays, holidays, and achievements; where difficult conversations have taken place and reconciliations have been made; where we've laughed until we cried and found comfort in times of sorrow. Each scratch and dent in the wood tells its own story, every mark from my sons' prolific artistic pens, and each stain holds a memory. This poor table itself has been through some things and is a constant through the ever-changing seasons of life, a place of stability in an often unstable world.

The table connects us to the grand story of humanity and the divine. It reminds us that we are part of something much larger than ourselves— a global and spiritual community that spans time and geography.

Whether we are aware of it or not, every time we sit down at a table, we are participating in this larger narrative. We are connected to the countless generations who have come before us, who have gathered around tables just like ours to share in the sacred act of eating together. We are also connected to the divine, who meets us at the table, offering us not just food, but grace, love, and the promise of His presence.

The table isn't just a place to put food; it's a symbol of provision and abundance, reflecting the generosity of the Provider. Sharing a meal is an act of trust, gratitude, and communion, whether viewed through a religious or secular lens.

As we gather around tables, we're part of a tradition that spans history, connecting us with deeper meanings in our everyday lives. In this book, I'll delve into the rich symbolism of the table, exploring it through the lens of the covenant of provision—a theme that's as nourishing for the soul as a great meal is for the body!

From one angle, the table reminds us that every situation has multiple perspectives—just as a table has different sides. We can sit at the same table and see things differently, reminding us that understanding and empathy are as vital as the food we share.

From another perspective, this table encourages us to nourish our bodies with wholesome food, just as it invites us to lead lives of authenticity and integrity. The meals served here aren't just about filling our stomachs; they're about feeding our souls, with food prepared in love and shared in truth.

But the table doesn't stop there. It teaches us that true nourishment comes from more than just what we eat—it's about the experiences we gather, the conversations we have, and the memories we make. Each meal is a chance to connect, to grow, and to savor both the physical sustenance and the richness of meaningful moments.

Because extra accessories often slow down the breakfast routine when my wife is trying to hustle the boys out the door for school, she enforces a simple rule: no iPads or backpacks bursting with their latest art projects at the table. Breakfast should be quick and focused—a tactical strike rather than a leisurely meander. But on those rare, slower-paced mornings, when the rush gives way to a more relaxed rhythm, she lets the rules slide, allowing the boys to indulge in their little luxuries. Of course, this often leads to a bigger mess. On those days, it feels like the boys bring more to the table than they take away, cluttering not just the space but the moment itself.

This brings to mind a story of a man who was once asked, *"What did you gain by regularly praying to God?"* The man responded, *"Nothing. But let me tell you what I lost: anger, ego, greed, depression, insecurity, and fear of death."* His answer reminds us of a profound truth: sometimes, the greatest answers to our prayers aren't about gaining but losing. And in that loss, there is true gain.

We often think of the table as a place where we come to receive—whether it's food, conversation, or comfort. But more often than not, the table is also a sacred place where we are invited to release. It's where we set down the burdens we've been carrying, where we leave behind our cluttered thoughts and anxieties, and where we empty ourselves of the distractions that weigh us down. Just like those mornings when the boys' art projects and gadgets make more of a mess than they do a masterpiece, we, too, sometimes bring too much unnecessary baggage to the table of our lives.

Imagine if we approached our spiritual tables the way my wife handles breakfast on a rushed morning—focused and uncluttered, stripping away the non-essentials so we can nourish ourselves with what truly matters. In a world that tells us to always seek more—more stuff, more status, more noise—there is something refreshingly liberating about a table where less is more. Where the goal isn't to fill ourselves up with all that the world has to offer but to make room for the divine to enter in.

So next time you pull up a chair, ask yourself not just what you're hoping to receive but also what you're willing to let go of. Because maybe, just maybe, the greatest blessings come not from what we add to the table but from what we're brave enough to leave behind.

And finally, this table stands as a sacred place, a meeting point between the earthly and the divine. It connects us to God, our Creator, as we break bread and give thanks. But it also connects us to each other, grounding us in our shared humanity and reminding us that in every meal, every gathering, we are discovering not just the flavors of life, but the essence of what it means to be truly alive.

So, the table is more than just wood and nails; it's a symbol of perspective, nourishment, connection, and spirituality—a place where life happens in all its fullness.

~Why Should I Read a Book About a Table? ~

We live in a world obsessed with transactions. In our relationships, careers, and even social interactions, we are constantly confronted with the question: "What do you bring to the table?" It's a question that seems innocent enough on the surface, but beneath it lies a pervasive reality: it is not just a casual inquiry—it's a test, a measure of one's worth based on what they can offer. And so, we spend a significant portion of our lives taking stock of ourselves, inventorying our skills, weighing our potential, and evaluating our value, all while silently wondering, "Am I good enough to earn a seat at the right table?" This relentless self-assessment is exhausting, and for many, it often feels like there's no table where they truly belong—a place where they can simply be without constantly proving their worth.

But what if there was a different kind of table? A table where the question isn't, "What do you bring?" but rather, "Are you hungry?" Imagine a table where your worth isn't tied to your credentials, your network, or your status, but is inherent in your desire to be present, to connect, and to be nourished. A table where there's always room for one more—a table designed specifically for you. No need to elbow your way in, no need to constantly prove yourself, and no need to worry about losing your place or being outperformed by the person sitting next to you.

This is precisely the kind of table this book is about. It's not just any table; it's a sacred space—a place of grace, rest, and abundant provision. It's the table where God meets you exactly as you are, and where you are invited to experience a deep, soul-nourishing communion. It's not a table found in a corner office, a prestigious social club, or even at the trendiest restaurant in town. This table is different because it is where your true self is not only welcomed but celebrated.

In these pages, I want to invite you to consider what it truly means to sit at this table. To sit down, relax, and know that you don't have to be anything more than who you already are. Here, there are no tests, no qualifications, no resumes to submit, and no hidden agendas. It's a place where you can lay down the burdens of performance and simply be. It's a place where you are seen, known, and loved, not for what you can produce or provide, but simply because you are.

This book is an invitation to discover the profound truth that the Creator of the universe has prepared a table for you. A table where you can meet God and have your deepest needs met by Him—a table where fellowship with others becomes a means of revealing the fullness of your humanity and the richness of genuine community. So, pull up a chair, my friend. There's a seat waiting for you, and I promise you—it's a place where you truly belong.

Yet, this journey to God's table requires discernment. It requires the courage to recognize when you're sitting at the wrong table. The elders used to say, *"You can't eat at everyone's table. You'll get indigestion."* And they were right. Not every table is meant for you. Some tables are filled with anxiety, insecurity, and the never-ending demand to prove yourself. Some tables, no matter how ornate or attractive, will leave you feeling empty. Better to admit that you walked through the wrong door than to spend your life in the wrong room, at the wrong table, trying to satisfy your soul with what will never truly nourish it.

If you find yourself at the wrong table, have the courage to stand up and remove yourself. And thankfully, sometimes, even when we don't have the courage to move, God removes us from some tables we formerly sat at to save us from a host who was serving poison.. There is an abundance waiting for you, but it lies at the table that God has prepared. It's a table where you don't have to fight for a seat, and where every bite is a blessing. Moving to that table might require a step of faith, a moment of clarity, and sometimes even the breaking of old patterns and comforts. But it is at that table where you will discover your true blessing.

That's the point of this book: to point you in the right direction—toward God's table. A table of divine invitation, where you don't just eat, but you are filled. Where you don't just sit, but you find rest. Where you don't just survive, but you truly thrive. Here, you are not asked to bring anything other than yourself, to be open to the abundance that awaits, and to allow God's grace to flow over you, through you, and around you. This table is already set. All you have to do is accept the invitation and take your place. So, come. There's a seat waiting for you.

At His table of Provision, Grace and Mercy,

Jermaine E. Pennington, D.Min.
Pastor/Teacher

Chapter 1
The Covenant

For over 40 years, I've been a follower of Christ, and for more than 30 of those years, I've been in ministry. And yet, here's a bit of a humbling confession: my understanding of God had some real gaps. I mean, how could that be? Well, like many in the Western church, I was conditioned by a faith tradition that, though rich in some ways, has its blind spots. One of the biggest? Our thin grasp of the word "covenant."

Here's the deal: to really know God—like, to truly understand God's divine nature—we've got to dive deep into this whole covenant thing. But if you grew up like me, Western culture doesn't give the word "covenant" the depth of meaning it deserves. It's not just a fancy way of saying "contract" or "deal." No, the biblical idea of covenant is something else entirely—way more serious and way more beautiful.

Why do we miss this? Part of it is because the Bible was written in a world that operated on different terms than we do now. Back then, in ancient cultures, a covenant wasn't just a pinky swear or a handshake—it was a life-and-death kind of deal. Blood, sacrifice, loyalty—this stuff was deep. Relationships, nations, and, most importantly, God's relationship with His people were built on covenants. But fast forward to our world today, where everything's fast-paced and transactional, and that kind of depth feels...distant, almost out of place.

Our language doesn't help either. Over time, the richness of the word "covenant" got watered down into simpler, weaker terms like "contract" or "agreement." Now, contracts are all about legal obligations, but a covenant? A covenant is about life, loyalty, and love. You can break a contract and walk away, but a covenant with God? It's eternal, even when we mess up.

Another thing that trips us up is our culture. We've drifted away from a communal, spiritual mindset to one that's all about me, myself, and I. We're taught to be independent, to go solo, and prioritize our personal success over community well-being. So the idea of living in a covenant—

a deep, committed bond with God and with each other—feels, well, kind of foreign, even a little intimidating. But the truth is, covenant life calls us to something bigger than ourselves. It's about shared identity, collective responsibility, and sacrificial love.

Let's be honest—words like "communal living" can make folks squirm. It brings to mind thoughts of forced sharing, giving up personal freedom, and gasp—"Socialism," or even worse, "Communism," which might as well be curse words in our capitalistic culture. But here's the kicker: the early church in the Book of Acts was all about it. They didn't just talk about covenant living—they actually lived it out, sharing their lives, their stuff, and their faith. And get this—it wasn't a burden. It was a joy. They weren't focused on individual success but on collective flourishing, showing the world a glimpse of what God's Kingdom really looks like.

I know, this might be the part where you're ready to close the book and walk away from the table. Believe me, I get it. But stick with me a little longer. There's a bigger, deeper picture here—one that just might surprise you.

So what are we missing when we lose sight of covenant? A lot! We miss out on the fullness of what it means to be in a relationship with God and each other. Covenant living is about depth—legal, moral, spiritual. It's about breaking free from the shallow, "me first" mentality that Western culture pushes and embracing the kind of life that God designed for us—a life of connection, responsibility, and love.

Which brings me to the symbol of the table. In the Bible, the table isn't just a spot to grab a meal—it's where covenants are made and renewed. It's where we experience God's provision and come together as one people. Think about it: the table is more than a piece of furniture. It's a sacred space where heaven meets earth. Yes, you heard that right. The table symbolizes a divine encounter, a moment where we're supported by God's covenant of provision.

At the table, we're reminded of God's faithfulness—His unbreakable promise to provide and protect. And here's the best part: we don't sit at this table as isolated individuals. We sit as a covenant community, united by our shared faith and identity in Christ. It's a place where the lines between "me" and "we" start to blur, and we begin to reflect the love and care God pours out on us.

So, as I keep unpacking what covenant really means, I want to invite you on this journey with me. Let's rediscover this life-changing, foundational concept that has the power to transform our understanding of God and our entire way of living. The covenant challenges us to live differently—to move beyond the "me first" mindset and embrace the deep, communal love that reflects God's faithfulness. It's a call to the table, where we are fed, renewed, and sent out to be a blessing to the world. Now, that's an invitation worth taking.

~The Power of a Covenant~

Several years ago, a friend of mine bought a new home in this trendy, gated subdivision where all the houses look like they were cut from the same cookie-cutter. He was so excited giving me the grand tour, and I could hear the passion in his voice as he talked about his new neighborhood. Then, he casually mentioned there was another house for sale and tried to rope me into being his neighbor. But I had a few reservations about this idea:

> 1. I prefer old homes with character—you know, the ones with creaky floors, quirky charm, and big, overgrown trees that obscure the view of passerby's, providing privacy. Those cookie-cutter homes? Not my thing.
>
> 2. The price tag was way out of my league—like, I would've had to do some either immoral or illegal things to afford to live in that neighborhood.
>
> 3. The house was in a "covenant community." Those places always rub me the wrong way with their nosy neighborhood watch programs and a million rules about how you can use your property. I mean, come on! I turn my nose up at covenants

designed to maintain uniformity. The whole thing screams "Stepford Wives" to me.

Plus, these neighborhoods have this knack for everyone being all up in your business. Not my style at all. Before I got married, I lived in my house for 10 years and didn't even know my neighbors' names. I'd mastered the art of the friendly-but-sterile wave to keep interactions minimal. Occasionally, I'd get caught in the yard, and they'd try to chat me up, but I'd always keep it short and sweet.

Then, along came my wife, Sara—the ultimate social butterfly. She made it her mission not just to meet our neighbors but to know them well. There's Mark, who spends most of his time outside stargazing with his telescope or detailing his truck, and his wife Babs (I'm not sure what she's in to because she's an introvert like me). Then there's Michael, the shirtless 80-year-old man with a chiseled body who is obsessed with having the most manicured lawn in the neighborhood. "Odd" Todd hosts weekly Trekkie parties, Laurie is the super friendly neighbor who constantly borrows things but she's also very generous, leaving gifts for us all the time, and Diana and her husband Sean have become my wife's neighborhood besties, regularly coming over for gatherings. For my introverted self, this has been very bothersome. Instead of enjoying my peaceful solitude, I'm constantly dragged into socializing and small talk. It's an extrovert's dream and an introvert's worst nightmare!

So, when I hear the word "covenant," my first instinct is to cringe a little—blame it on my Western cultural upbringing! You see, I'm a bit of a selfish loner, not exactly the poster child for community living. I'm generous when it comes to sharing my money, stuff and other earthly resources, but I fiercely guard my time and personal space. This mindset makes experiencing the power of covenant a bit of a challenge.

A covenant isn't just any old promise; it's like a supercharged, sacred agreement with bells and whistles! It's a binding, enduring pledge that packs a serious punch in terms of power, responsibility and community. Unlike your everyday agreements, covenants are steeped in history, spirituality, and culture, often carrying deep implications for those who enter into them. To truly appreciate covenants, we need to dive into their nature, historical and spiritual significance, and their transformative impact on individuals and communities.

In our society, breaking an agreement is as easy as catching a cold. People are often ready to bail at the first hint of trouble. This "me-first" mentality is a real bummer for holding together our churches, families, marriages—you name it. But covenants? They play by a whole different set of rules. Covenants are serious and binding, involving commitments that aren't easily broken. They're all about depth and dedication. Many traditions surround covenants with rituals, symbols, or ceremonies, emphasizing their importance and the serious commitment of those involved. This solemn vibe sets covenants apart from your typical contracts or agreements.

Throughout history, covenants have been total game-changers, shaping societies and relationships in big ways. In ancient times, they were used to form alliances, settle disputes, and outline social or legal obligations. For example, in biblical times, covenants were at the core of the relationship between God and the people of Israel, laying down the law for religious and ethical conduct.

Take the covenant between God and Abraham—this was a big deal! It set the stage for the Israelites as God's chosen people, showing the world how God wants to interact with humanity. This covenant came with promises of land, descendants, and blessings and required Abraham and his crew to follow certain commandments and practices.

In many religious traditions, covenants are seen as sacred commitments involving not just the people involved but also the divine. This spiritual layer adds extra weight and accountability since covenants are often believed to be overseen by a higher power. This isn't just about mutual benefit; it's about fulfilling a divine purpose or calling.

For instance, in Christianity, the New Covenant through Jesus Christ is like the ultimate upgrade, fulfilling and expanding earlier covenants. It offers salvation and a direct relationship with God to all who believe, focusing on grace, redemption, and the transformation of individuals and communities. A lot of this book will focus on that particular covenant.

Covenants have the power to transform individuals and communities by setting a framework for relationships, responsibilities, and shared values. They often call for specific actions, behaviors, or beliefs, leading to personal and collective growth. The binding nature of covenants fosters a sense of accountability and trust, as everyone is expected to uphold their commitments.

Moreover, covenants can inspire hope and purpose. For individuals, being part of a covenant can provide a sense of belonging and direction. For communities, covenants can be a foundation for unity and cooperation, helping navigate challenges and conflicts.

The true power of a covenant lies in its ability to create deep, lasting connections that go beyond simple agreements. By exploring the historical and spiritual significance of covenants, we gain a deeper understanding of their transformative potential. Whether in religious, social, or personal contexts, covenants shape our identities, guide our actions, and connect us to something greater than ourselves. They remind us of the enduring power of commitment and the profound impact that shared promises can have on our lives and the world around us. The covenant is the reminder that God keeps His Word and His Word is a love letter to His people.

~How Our Covenant Was Created~

I vividly remember the days following the tragic events of 9/11. A close friend of mine, Pastor Al Ward was trying to help his very young son make sense of the chaos. His son, feeling as if his entire world had been attacked, watched his sense of security, protection, and provision crumble like the Twin Towers. With deep concern, his son asked him, *"Dad, what's going to happen to me?"* My friend looked into his son's eyes and, with all the love and determination in his heart, reassured him, *"Son, as long as I'm alive, you'll never have to worry about what you'll eat, where you'll sleep, or whether you'll be safe. Taking care of those things is my job."*

My friend meant every word, and his promise was filled with the deep, unwavering commitment of a father's love. But as strong as that love is, no earthly parent can guarantee with absolute certainty that they can always fulfill such a promise. Life is unpredictable, and there are forces beyond our control. Yet, there is one who can—and does—make such a promise with absolute certainty: our Heavenly Father.

God's promise to take care of us is not limited by the uncertainties of this world. It is a covenant, unbreakable and eternal, that He has made with us. Every time we gather at the table, we are reminded of this divine promise. The table is more than just a place where we share meals; it is a powerful symbol of God's unwavering commitment to provide, protect, and guide us through every storm. It stands as a reminder that no matter how the world around us may shake, our security in Him is steadfast. He promises to be our provider, our shelter, and our peace.

In times of fear and uncertainty, when our earthly sense of security is shaken, we can look to God's covenant with confidence. His love and care for us are not subject to the changing tides of this world. Unlike human promises, which can falter under pressure, God's promises are sure and unfailing. As we sit at the table, let it serve as a reminder that we are not alone. We are held in the loving hands of a Father who will never let us go, who will provide for us in ways beyond our imagination, and who assures us that in Him, we are always safe.

Our covenant of provision is like the ultimate promise from a loving Creator who guarantees to meet our needs. But this isn't just any old promise—it's a divine pledge rooted in love, sacrifice, and unwavering faithfulness. So, get ready, because we're about to dive into the origins of this covenant, exploring sacred texts and theological reflections to uncover its profound significance.

First up, the covenant of provision is all about the Creator's unconditional love for humanity. This isn't a "you scratch my back, I'll scratch yours" kind of deal—it's a relational bond built on deep, abiding love. The Creator didn't just set this up to keep things running smoothly;

it's about providing, protecting, and guiding us because of pure, infinite love.

In many religious traditions, this love is described as all-encompassing and boundless, stretching out grace and mercy to everyone. The covenant itself is a big ol' expression of this love, offering a promise that goes beyond our human flaws and limitations. It's like a divine safety net, reassuring us that the Creator's commitment to our well-being is rock-solid, even when we mess up.

Now, let's talk about the juicy bit—the element of sacrifice. In many sacred texts, covenants are often sealed with sacrifices, which underline the seriousness and sanctity of the agreement. In the Judeo-Christian tradition, this reaches its peak with the life and death of Jesus Christ, seen as the mediator of the New Covenant. This ultimate act of love and redemption isn't just a grand gesture; it bridges the gap between humanity and the divine, showing just how far the Creator will go to fulfill the promise of provision and redemption. It's like the ultimate "I got your back" move!

The faithfulness of the Creator is the glue that holds this whole covenant together. Unlike human agreements that can be broken or renegotiated, this divine covenant is steadfast. The Creator's faithfulness is like a rock, providing assurance that the promises made will be kept, no matter what curveballs life throws. From the provision of manna in the wilderness to the protection of the Israelites and the promise of eternal life, these stories showcase the Creator's unwavering reliability.

Theologically speaking, this covenant of provision is like an open invitation to enter into a relationship with the Creator. It's not just about getting what we need to survive; it covers all aspects of life, including spiritual and emotional well-being. It's like a VIP pass to align our lives with a higher purpose and moral framework.

As part of this covenant, we're invited to respond with faith, trust, and obedience. It's a two-way street—while the Creator provides, we're called to live in line with the covenant's principles and values. This dynamic dance fosters spiritual growth and transformation, drawing us closer to the divine.

In essence, our covenant of provision is a profound testament to the Creator's love, sacrifice, and faithfulness. It's a divine promise that extends beyond just sustenance to encompass every part of our lives. By exploring its origins through sacred texts and theological reflections, we get a deeper understanding of its significance and the transformative power it holds. This covenant isn't just a contract; it's an invitation to enter into a relationship with the Creator, filled with trust, faith, and the assurance of provision.

From the dawn of creation, the narrative of humanity's relationship with God has been one marked by covenants—sacred agreements that bind us to Him in a relationship of love, trust, and faithfulness. These covenants are not mere contracts or legal agreements; they are profound expressions of God's unwavering commitment to His creation. In Scripture, we see that God established covenants with humanity to reveal His character, to guide us in our journey through life, and to assure us of His eternal promises. Understanding what God did through these covenants and why it matters is key to grasping the depth of His love and the certainty of His faithfulness.

God's Covenant with Creation: The Foundation of All Relationships
The first covenant God made was with all of creation. In Genesis, after the flood, God made a covenant with Noah, his descendants, and every living creature, promising never again to destroy the earth by floodwaters. This covenant was marked by the sign of the rainbow, a perpetual reminder of God's mercy and faithfulness (Genesis 9:8-17). This covenant established the foundation for all relationships—between God and humanity, humanity and creation, and humanity with itself. It underscores that God is deeply invested in His creation, committed to its flourishing, and willing to enter into binding agreements that protect and sustain it.

This matters because it sets the tone for all of God's interactions with humanity. It shows us that God is not distant or detached from His creation; instead, He is actively involved, seeking to establish a world where life can thrive under His care and guidance. This covenant reveals God's desire for a world in which His creation is secure, protected, and valued.

Confusion about the covenants in Scripture is common and often leads to misunderstandings about how God relates to us today. Many people mistakenly see the covenants as one continuous agreement, missing the unique purposes of each. This blending can obscure the New Covenant in Christ, causing confusion about our relationship with God and His promises. The confusion deepens when we read phrases like *"I have made an everlasting covenant with you."* The Hebrew word for "everlasting," Olam (עולם), doesn't actually mean "forever" as we think of it—it usually refers to a set duration, lasting until God establishes a better promise.

The Problem of Overlapping Covenants
The various covenants in the Bible—such as the Noahic, Abrahamic, Mosaic, Davidic, and New Covenants—were given at different times and for different purposes. Each covenant had specific promises, requirements, and signs associated with it, and each played a unique role in God's unfolding plan for humanity.

When people confuse these covenants as one overarching agreement, they often fail to recognize the distinctiveness of each. For example, the Mosaic Covenant, given at Mount Sinai, included the Law, which governed Israel's life and relationship with God. This covenant was specific to the nation of Israel and included commandments, rituals, and sacrifices that were meant to set them apart as God's chosen people. However, this covenant was not intended to be eternal; it was a preparatory stage leading to something greater *(Refer to Hebrews 8:13)*.

On the other hand, the New Covenant, established through the death and resurrection of Jesus Christ, is fundamentally different. It is not based on the Law but on grace and faith. The New Covenant fulfills the promises of the previous covenants and extends God's relationship to all people, Jew and Gentile alike, through faith in Christ. When the distinctions between these covenants are not understood, people may mistakenly believe that the requirements of the Mosaic Law still apply to them, leading to a legalistic approach to faith that overlooks the grace offered in Christ.

The Mosaic Covenant vs. The New Covenant
A common confusion arises when people fail to distinguish between the Mosaic Covenant and the New Covenant. The Mosaic Covenant, with its emphasis on law and obedience, can sometimes be wrongly applied to Christians who live under the New Covenant of grace. For instance, some may believe that they must follow the Old Testament laws and rituals to be in right standing with God, not realizing that these were specific to Israel and were fulfilled in Christ.

The New Covenant, however, is centered on the person of Jesus Christ and the work of the Holy Spirit in the believer's life. It is based on the promise of internal transformation rather than external adherence to a set of laws. The New Covenant brings a new way of relating to God, where faith in Christ, rather than the works of the Law, is the basis of our righteousness. By not recognizing this distinction, believers may fall into the trap of legalism, trying to earn God's favor through works rather than resting in the grace provided by Christ.

The Davidic Covenant and Misunderstandings of God's Kingdom
Another area of confusion can occur with the Davidic Covenant, where God promised David that his throne would be established forever. Some people mistakenly conflate this with the notion that the physical nation of Israel or a specific political kingdom must be restored for God's promises to be fulfilled. However, the New Testament reveals that Jesus Christ is the fulfillment of the Davidic Covenant, reigning as the eternal King in a spiritual kingdom that transcends earthly nations.

When this covenant is misunderstood, people may focus on earthly power and political dominion, missing the reality that God's kingdom is not of this world but is manifested in the hearts and lives of those who follow Christ. Understanding that Christ fulfills the Davidic Covenant in a way that establishes an eternal, spiritual kingdom helps clarify our role as citizens of God's kingdom, which is marked by love, justice, and peace rather than political power.

The Importance of Understanding the New Covenant

The New Covenant is the covenant that applies to us today, and it is essential for Christians to understand its significance. Unlike the previous covenants, which were often conditional and required specific actions or obedience to the Law, the New Covenant is based on the finished work of Jesus Christ. It offers forgiveness of sins, the indwelling of the Holy Spirit, and a personal relationship with God.

When believers understand the New Covenant, they recognize that their standing with God is not based on their ability to follow the Law but on their faith in Christ. This understanding frees them from the burden of trying to earn God's favor and allows them to live in the freedom and grace that Christ provides. It also empowers them to live out their faith in a way that reflects the love and justice of God, knowing that they are part of a new creation where *old things have passed away and all things have become new* (2 Corinthians 5:17).

Why This Matters

Understanding the differences between the covenants is essential for accurately interpreting Scripture and understanding our relationship with God. Recognizing that the New Covenant is the one that applies to us today allows us to fully embrace the grace, freedom, and transformation it offers. This clarity helps us avoid legalism, misinterpreting Scripture, and confusion about God's promises. Without this understanding, many Christians end up living a fragmented, inconsistent faith that doesn't align with biblical truth.

By clearly distinguishing between the covenants, we can better appreciate the richness of God's plan for humanity and how He has progressively revealed Himself throughout history. We can see how each covenant served a purpose in leading to the ultimate fulfillment in Christ and how we, as believers, are now partakers of the New Covenant's blessings. This clarity strengthens our faith, deepens our relationship with God, and equips us to live out our calling as His people in a way that honors the true intent of His Word.

Moreover, understanding the distinctions between the covenants allows us to grasp the continuity and consistency of God's character and promises. Each covenant reveals a different aspect of God's relationship with humanity—His justice in the covenant with Noah, His faithfulness in the covenant with Abraham, His holiness in the covenant with Moses, and His kingship in the covenant with David. All these covenants find their ultimate expression and fulfillment in the New Covenant, established through the life, death, and resurrection of Jesus Christ. Recognizing this divine progression not only illuminates the unity of Scripture but also encourages us to trust in the unchanging nature of God, who keeps His promises and works all things according to His redemptive plan. This understanding empowers us to live with confidence and hope, knowing that we are part of an unfolding story that began long before us and will continue into eternity.

~*The Benefits and Specifics of Our Covenant*~

I recently introduced my sons to one of my all-time favorite childhood cult classics—Flash Gordon. As they watched, they couldn't help but crack up at the gloriously ridiculous, second-rate special effects that were a masterpiece of their time. The deep belly laughs came quickly, but they were also hooked by the plot's nonstop action and unapologetically cheesy drama. Then, we hit the grand finale. Just as the credits rolled, the screen flashed: "The End?"—complete with a question mark and the sinister echo of Ming the Merciless' laughter. Had he really died? Was this a sly promise of a sequel? I told my sons that this unresolved mystery has haunted me since 1980 when the movie first hit theaters. They wholeheartedly agreed: more than 40 years of suspense is just plain cruel—the agony of waiting, longing, and never getting closure.

Now, imagine waiting not just decades, but thousands of years for the promise of a coming Messiah. And when He finally arrives, bringing with Him a New Covenant of grace, some can hardly believe it. They cling to the old ways, still prisoners of an expired promise, unable or unwilling to embrace the fulfillment standing right in front of them. It's like getting the answer to a lifelong question but refusing to believe it's true. After all that waiting, why on earth would you pass up such a gift?

Holding onto the Old Covenant when the new has come is like the man on a long flight from New York to Los Angeles, sitting next to his neighbor who feasted on steak, lobster, Dom Pérignon, and Crème Brûlée, while he sat nibbling on stale peanuts and sipping tap water. Finally, after hours of enduring this torment, he leaned over and asked his neighbor how he managed to afford such exquisite dining. With a smile, the neighbor replied, *"Oh, it was all included with the flight!"* Suddenly, his empty stomach groaned as he realized just how much he missed out on.

Like this hungry passenger, many of us are on a journey where we're missing out on the abundant blessings that are already paid for. We've been so focused on the old menu that we've completely overlooked the gourmet feast that comes with the ticket. Why settle for peanuts when there's a banquet waiting for you? Don't let old expectations blind you to the new delights that are already yours—pull up a chair, dig in, and savor every bite of what's been prepared for you.

"The table is a meeting place, a gathering ground, the source of sustenance and nourishment, festivity, safety, and satisfaction. A person cooking is a person giving: Even the simplest food is a gift" are the beautiful words written by Laurie Colwin and they captures the profound significance of the table in our lives. The table is not just a piece of furniture; it is a symbol of connection, community, and care. It is where we come together, not only to eat but to share our lives, to celebrate, and to find comfort and security in the presence of others.

The table is a meeting place, where people from different walks of life come together, united by the simple act of sharing a meal. It is where stories are told, relationships are built, and bonds are strengthened. Around the table, we find common ground, regardless of our differences. It is a space where we are reminded of our shared humanity, where the barriers that divide us can be set aside, even if just for a moment.

At its most basic level, the table is where we find sustenance and nourishment. The food laid before us provides the energy and nutrients we need to survive and thrive. But Colwin reminds us that the nourishment we receive at the table goes beyond the physical. The act of sharing a meal with others nourishes our souls as well. It is an opportunity to connect with those around us, to engage in meaningful conversation, and to experience the warmth of companionship.

The food itself, whether it's a simple bowl of soup or a lavish feast, is a gift. The person who prepares the meal is giving more than just food; they are offering their time, effort, and care. Cooking is an act of love, a way of expressing care and concern for others. Even the simplest food, prepared with love, becomes a symbol of that care, a tangible expression of the giver's desire to nurture and support those they are feeding.

The table is also a place of festivity and celebration. It is where we gather to mark special occasions, to celebrate milestones, and to create memories that will last a lifetime. Whether it's a birthday, a holiday, or a simple dinner with loved ones, the table is where we come together to rejoice and give thanks for the blessings in our lives.

The rituals and traditions associated with the table—setting it, saying grace, sharing stories—enhance the sense of occasion and add to the joy of the moment. The table becomes a stage for the celebration of life's joys, both big and small. It is where we toast to the future, reflect on the past, and savor the present.

Finally, the table is a place of safety and satisfaction. It is where we find comfort and security, knowing that our needs will be met and that we are cared for. The familiarity of the table, the routine of shared meals, provides a sense of stability in an often chaotic world. It is a place where we can relax, be ourselves, and feel at home.

The satisfaction we experience at the table is not just about the food; it is about the sense of fulfillment that comes from being part of a community, from knowing that we are loved and that we belong. It is a satisfaction that nourishes not just our bodies, but our hearts and minds as well.

Colwin's observation that *"a person cooking is a person giving"* highlights the selfless nature of preparing a meal. Cooking is an act of generosity, an offering of oneself for the benefit of others. It requires time, effort, and often, a great deal of thought and care. The cook thinks about the preferences and needs of those they are feeding, choosing ingredients, and preparing dishes that will bring comfort, joy, and satisfaction.

Even the simplest food, prepared with love and intention, becomes a gift. It is a way of saying, "I care about you. I want to nourish you. I want to see you satisfied and happy." This act of giving is powerful, as it fosters connection, strengthens relationships, and builds a sense of community.

In this way, the table and the act of cooking become much more than just means of sustenance. They are acts of love, care, and connection. They are ways of building and nurturing relationships, of creating a sense of belonging, and of expressing care and concern for others. In a world that often feels disconnected and fragmented, the table and the food shared upon it are reminders of our shared humanity and the power of giving.

Laurie Colwin's reflections remind us that the table is a sacred space, where life's most important moments unfold. It is where we find sustenance and nourishment, festivity and celebration, safety and satisfaction. It is a place where the simple act of cooking becomes a profound act of giving, where even the simplest food becomes a gift of love. As we gather around the table, let us remember the power of this space to connect us, to nourish us, and to bring us together in a spirit of love and generosity. The table God has established in our lives is set with many great benefits including:

1. Provision for Physical Needs

The covenant assures that our physical needs will be met. This includes the necessities of life such as food, shelter, and clothing. The promise of provision is a central theme in many religious texts, where the Creator is depicted as a provider and sustainer.

Scriptural Reference:

- Matthew 6:31-33 (NIV)"*So do not worry, saying, 'What shall we eat?' or 'What shall we drink?' or 'What shall we wear?' For the pagans run after all these things, and your heavenly Father knows that you need them. But seek first his kingdom and his righteousness, and all these things will be given to you as well.*"

- This passage highlights the assurance that when we prioritize our spiritual lives, our material needs will also be taken care of.

- A testimony might include someone sharing how they experienced unexpected provision during a difficult financial period, reinforcing the belief in a caring and responsive divine presence.

Your Personal Testimony of Provision:

_____

_____

_____

_____

_____

2. Spiritual Nourishment and Growth

Beyond physical needs, the covenant provides for our spiritual nourishment. It offers guidance, wisdom, and the means to grow in our faith deepening our understanding, inviting us into a relationship rooted in commitment, promoting accountability and fostering community and shared identity. This aspect of the covenant helps believers develop a deeper relationship with the Creator and experience spiritual growth.

Scriptural Reference:

- Psalm 23:1-3 (NIV) *"The Lord is my shepherd, I lack nothing. He makes me lie down in green pastures, he leads me beside quiet waters, He refreshes my soul. He guides me along the right paths for his name's sake."*

- This psalm portrays the Creator as a shepherd who cares for and nourishes the soul, providing rest, guidance, and spiritual refreshment.

- A testimony might include an individual describing how they found spiritual guidance and peace during a period of confusion or turmoil, attributing this clarity to their faith in the covenant.

Your Personal Testimony of Spiritual Growth:

_____
_____
_____
_____
_____

3. Peace and Joy

The covenant brings peace and joy, transcending circumstances. This peace is often described as a sense of tranquility and confidence that comes from trusting in the Creator's provision and faithfulness. The joy is a deep, abiding happiness that is not dependent on external conditions but derives from an otherworldly Source.

Scriptural Reference:

- Philippians 4:6-7 (NIV) *"Do not be anxious about anything, but in every situation, by prayer and petition, with thanksgiving, present your requests to God. And the peace of God, which transcends all understanding, will guard your hearts and your minds in Christ Jesus."*
- This passage emphasizes the peace that comes from relying on divine provision and being thankful for the blessings received.
- A testimony might include an account of finding peace and joy in the midst of a challenging situation, such as illness or loss, by leaning on the covenant's promises.

Your Personal Testimony of Peace and Joy:

_____
_____
_____
_____
_____

The Table Book   Jermaine E. Pennington

4. Eternal Hope

One of the most profound benefits of the covenant is the promise of eternal hope. This aspect assures believers of a future beyond this life, offering a sense of purpose and destiny. It provides comfort and motivation, knowing that life has an eternal dimension and that there is hope beyond present struggles.

Scriptural Reference:

- John 14:2-3 (NIV) *"My Father's house has many rooms; if that were not so, would I have told you that I am going there to prepare a place for you? And if I go and prepare a place for you, I will come back and take you to be with me that you also may be where I am."*

- This passage speaks to the promise of eternal life and the assurance of a place in the divine presence.

- A testimony might involve an individual sharing how the promise of eternal life provides them with hope and courage, particularly in facing mortality or the loss of loved ones.

Your Personal Testimony of Eternal Hope:

_____
_____
_____
_____
_____

The covenant of provision offers a comprehensive promise that covers all aspects of our lives—physical, spiritual, emotional, and eternal. It assures us of our needs being met, provides a foundation for spiritual growth, brings peace and joy, and offers a hope that transcends this life. Through scriptural references and personal testimonies, we see how this covenant profoundly impacts those who embrace it, offering assurance and guidance in every aspect of their journey. We do well to study the covenant of provision in order to gain a better understanding of the heart of the Giver.

~How Do We Enter into the Covenant? ~

Entering into the covenant of provision is more than just acknowledging a divine promise; it's an invitation to step into a sacred relationship that calls for both acceptance and unwavering faith. This covenant, a gift from the Creator, isn't something we earn or negotiate; it's freely offered, waiting for us to open our hearts and hands to receive it. But to truly embrace this covenant is to do more than just accept it intellectually—it requires us to weave it into the very fabric of our lives, letting it shape our actions, our thoughts, and our outlook on life.

At its core, the covenant of provision is about trusting in the Creator's promises, believing that we are cared for, loved, and provided for in ways that transcend our human understanding. It's about recognizing that our needs—whether they are physical, emotional, or spiritual—are known by God, and that He has already made provision for them. This trust isn't passive; it's active, dynamic, and rooted in a deep relationship with the Divine. It calls us to look beyond the visible, to see with eyes of faith, and to rest in the assurance that we are never abandoned, never left without what we truly need.

But this covenant also invites us to a deeper commitment. Embracing it fully involves more than just a mental ascent; it requires us to commit our lives to the principles and practices that align us with God's will and ways. This might mean cultivating a life of prayer, where we regularly communicate with God, bringing our needs before Him and listening for His guidance. It could involve the practice of gratitude, where we actively acknowledge and give thanks for the ways God provides, even in the smallest details of our lives.

Moreover, entering this covenant often means adopting a lifestyle of stewardship. Recognizing that everything we have comes from God, we are called to manage our resources—whether they be time, talents, or treasures—with wisdom and generosity. This is not about hoarding for ourselves, but about living with an open hand, willing to share and bless others, trusting that as we give, God will continue to meet our needs abundantly.

Ultimately, the covenant of provision is a journey of deepening trust and growing relationship. It's about learning to rely not on our own understanding or efforts, but on the faithfulness of a God who promises to supply all our needs according to His riches in glory. As we accept this covenant and commit to living it out, we find ourselves not just recipients of divine provision, but participants in the unfolding of God's generosity in the world. It's a life marked by peace, confidence, and the unshakeable belief that in every circumstance, God's provision is enough. This section outlines the practical steps and spiritual practices necessary for entering into and living within the covenant.

1. Acceptance of the Covenant

The first step to entering the covenant is acceptance. This means recognizing and acknowledging the covenant's existence and its significance in our lives. Acceptance involves an open-hearted willingness to receive the covenant's promises and the responsibilities that come with it.

Practical Step: Reflect on the Covenant

- Spend time reflecting on the meaning and implications of the covenant. Consider how it aligns with your beliefs, values, and life experiences. Reflect on your willingness to accept this gift and the changes it might bring to your life.

_____
_____
_____
_____
_____

- Engage in prayer or meditation to seek clarity and understanding about the covenant. Ask for guidance and a heart open to accepting the covenant's terms. This practice helps to center your thoughts and intentions, preparing you to fully embrace the covenant.

_____
_____
_____
_____

2. Faith and Trust

Entering the covenant also requires faith and trust in the Creator's promises. Faith involves believing in the unseen and trusting that the covenant's promises will be fulfilled. This trust is fundamental to the relationship established by the covenant.

Practical Step: Affirmation of Faith

- Make a personal affirmation of your faith and trust in the covenant. This could be a written statement, a verbal declaration, or a quiet commitment in your heart. This affirmation solidifies your intention to live in alignment with the covenant.

_____
_____
_____
_____

Spiritual Practice: Reading Sacred Texts

- Regularly read and reflect on sacred texts that discuss the covenant and the Creator's promises. This practice helps to strengthen your faith and trust by providing a deeper understanding of the covenant's foundations and assurances.

_____
_____
_____

3. Commitment to the Covenant

Entering the covenant involves a commitment to live according to its principles and values. This means being willing to follow the guidance provided by the covenant, even when it is challenging and or inconvenient. Commitment to a covenant is growth by challenging our immaturity and childish desire to always have our way.

Practical Step: Setting Intentions

- Set specific intentions or goals that align with the covenant's principles. These could include committing to certain behaviors, practices, or attitudes that reflect the covenant's values, such as generosity, kindness, or humility.

Spiritual Practice: Regular Worship and Fellowship

- Participate in regular worship and fellowship with a community that shares your beliefs. This practice provides support, encouragement, and accountability as you commit to living according to the covenant.

4. Spiritual Practices for Growth

To fully embrace and live within the covenant, it is important to engage in ongoing spiritual practices that foster growth and deepen your relationship with the Creator.

Practical Step: Daily Reflection and Journaling

- Make time each day for reflection and journaling about your experiences and insights related to the covenant. This practice helps you stay mindful of your commitments and the ways the covenant is manifesting in your life.

_____
_____
_____
_____
_____

Spiritual Practice: Acts of Service

- Engage in acts of service to others as a way to live out the covenant's principles. Serving others not only benefits the community but also helps you embody the values of the covenant in practical ways.

_____
_____
_____
_____
_____

5. Seeking Guidance and Support

Finally, entering the covenant often involves seeking guidance and support from others who are also committed to the covenant. This can include mentors, spiritual leaders, or a faith community.

Practical Step: Find a Mentor or Spiritual Guide

- Identify a mentor or spiritual guide who can offer wisdom, guidance, and support as you navigate your journey with the covenant. This person can provide insights, answer questions, and help you stay focused on your spiritual path.

_____
_____
_____
_____
_____

Spiritual Practice: Community Involvement

- Become actively involved in a faith community that shares your commitment to the covenant. Being part of a supportive community provides encouragement and helps you grow in your understanding and practice of the covenant.

_____
_____
_____
_____
_____

Entering into the covenant of provision is a profound and life-changing decision. It requires acceptance, faith, commitment, and an ongoing engagement in spiritual practices. By following these steps and embracing these practices, you can fully enter into and live within the covenant, experiencing the peace, joy, and provision it promises. This journey is not just about receiving blessings but also about growing in faith and becoming a vessel of the covenant's values in the world.

Chapter 2
The Table is Spread

In Psalm 78:19-20, the Israelites, wandering in the wilderness, doubted God's ability to provide for them. *"They spoke against God; they said, 'Can God really spread a table in the wilderness? True, he struck the rock, and water gushed out, streams flowed abundantly, but can he also give us bread? Can he supply meat for his people?'"* These words reflect a profound moment of skepticism and fear, a questioning of God's power and faithfulness in the face of overwhelming need. Yet, this doubt stands in stark contrast to the reality of God's unwavering provision, a reality that has been experienced by countless generations, particularly those who have known the depths of oppression and lack. For these communities, God's provision is not a theoretical concept; it is a lived experience, a tangible reality that has been witnessed time and time again. The table is spread, and the feast of the Lord is ongoing, inviting all to partake in the abundance that only God can provide.

Throughout history, famine and scarcity have often given birth to the strength of the oppressed. Those who have faced deprivation, who have been marginalized and oppressed, have developed a unique understanding of God's provision. Their theology is not shaped by abundance but by lack, not by ease but by struggle. It is within these crucibles of suffering that a deep, unshakable faith is forged—a faith that sees beyond the immediate circumstances to the God who provides in the midst of the wilderness.

This is the context in which the phrase, *"God will make a way out of no way,"* finds its meaning. It is a declaration of faith that has been tested and proven in the fires of adversity. For those who have faced the harsh realities of life—whether it be slavery, poverty, discrimination, or exile—this phrase is more than just words. It is a proclamation of God's ability to provide, even when the situation seems hopeless. It is a testimony to the truth that God can, indeed, spread a table in the wilderness.

The unspeakable joy that arises from experiencing God's provision is something that cannot be fully understood until it is lived. For those who have seen God spread a table of abundance in the midst of scarcity, who have watched as God provided bread and meat when there seemed to be none, this joy is profound and all-encompassing. It is the joy of knowing that God is faithful, that He sees the needs of His people, and that He acts on their behalf.

This joy is not merely about the satisfaction of physical needs; it is about the deeper spiritual reality of God's presence and care. When God provides in the midst of lack, it is a reminder that He is with us, that He has not abandoned us, and that He is working for our good. It is a joy that comes from knowing that we are seen and loved by the Creator of the universe, who is intimately involved in the details of our lives.

The image of a table spread with abundance is a powerful one. It is a symbol of God's generosity, His hospitality, and His desire to bless His people. In the Bible, the table is often associated with fellowship, celebration, and covenant. It is where people come together to share in the blessings of God, to break bread and enjoy the fruit of His provision. The table is a place of inclusion, where all are invited to partake in the feast.

The invitation to come to the table, where the feast of the Lord is going on, is an invitation to experience God's provision in all its fullness. It is an invitation to move from doubt to faith, from fear to trust, and from scarcity to abundance. It is an invitation to witness firsthand the reality that God can and does provide, even in the most unlikely circumstances.

As we reflect on the idea of God spreading a table in the wilderness, we are reminded of His faithfulness throughout history. The same God who provided for the Israelites in the desert is the God who provides for us today. He is the God who makes a way out of no way, who spreads a table of abundance in the midst of scarcity, and who invites us all to come and partake in His blessings.

If you have not yet experienced the joy of God's provision, the invitation is open: *come on in where the table spread, and the feast of the Lord is going on*. Here, you will find not only physical sustenance but also spiritual nourishment, peace, and joy. Here, you will encounter the God who provides abundantly, who cares deeply, and who delights in blessing His people. The table is spread—come, and be filled.

~All My Favorite Foods~

Both of my sons are what you might call "culinary connoisseurs"—others might call them picky eaters, but let's stick with the more flattering term, shall we? When my mother visits, she often finds herself at a loss for words watching how little they seem to eat. It's a stark contrast to my own childhood, where dinner was a take-it-or-leave-it affair. My mother cooked one meal, and if you didn't like it, well, tough luck—you ate it anyway because the alternative was going hungry.

But my sons? They've got it good. They've managed to carve out their own little culinary kingdoms, where my poor wife finds herself preparing multiple dishes to cater to their specific tastes. And let's be honest, they're a bit spoiled. But here's the funny thing: when a meal finally does hit the sweet spot—think crab legs, macaroni, salmon, or fried chicken—they dive in with the enthusiasm of food critics at a five-star restaurant. Suddenly, the picky eaters become bottomless pits, doing little happy dances as they inhale every bite, barely pausing to breathe.

These moments remind me of a profound truth: God, our Heavenly Father, spreads a table before us filled with all our favorite foods. Jesus illustrated this beautifully when He said, "*Which of you, if your son asks for bread, will give him a stone? Or if he asks for a fish, will give him a snake? If you, then, though you are evil, know how to give good gifts to your children, how much more will your Father in heaven give good gifts to those who ask Him?*" (Matthew 7:9-11). This table, filled with their favorite dishes, is more than just a meal—it's a tangible expression of God's abundance and generosity. It's as if the Provider Himself knows every detail of our tastes, serving up dishes that not only meet our needs but also bring us deep joy. This feast, rich with flavors and delights, symbolizes the fullness of life, a testament to the blessings we receive through the covenant of provision. It serves as a powerful reminder that God provides for us with such care and love, giving us not just what we need, but what truly makes us joyful.

So, yes, my sons might be a little picky, but when they find what they love, they remind us all of the joy that comes from being truly satisfied. Their eyes light up, they do those little happy dances, and for a moment, all is right in their world. It's a simple pleasure, yet it's a powerful reminder of what it means to be truly satisfied. It's not just about filling their stomachs; it's about savoring the experience, relishing in the delight of having something that brings them genuine happiness—not just with food, but with the blessings that life, and the Provider, so generously offer.

In those moments, I'm reminded that this joy is a reflection of the deeper blessings that life, and our Divine Provider, so generously offer. Just as my sons' favorite meals are prepared with love and attention to detail, so too are the blessings in our lives thoughtfully provided by a Creator who knows us intimately—our needs, our desires, our quirks. When we find something that resonates with us, whether it's a meal, a relationship, a moment of peace, or a burst of inspiration, it's a taste of the abundant life that God promises.

These moments of satisfaction, as fleeting as they may seem, are glimpses of the fullness of life that God intends for us. They remind us that life's true joys aren't found in abundance for its own sake, but in the richness of experiences that touch our hearts and souls. Just as my sons find joy in their favorite foods, we too can find joy in the blessings that nourish not just our bodies, but our spirits. It's a reminder that God's generosity isn't just about meeting our needs; it's about delighting us, surprising us, and filling our lives with moments of pure, unadulterated joy.

So, while my sons may be a bit particular about what's on their plates, their enthusiasm for the things they love serves as a lesson for us all: to seek out and cherish those moments of true satisfaction, to recognize the hand of the Provider in the blessings we receive, and to celebrate the joy that comes from a life richly filled with love, grace, and abundance.

Symbolic Significance of the Feast:

1. Representation of Abundance

The feast before us carries profound symbolic meaning. It is a tangible expression of the covenant of provision, a reminder that God is our Provider, who meets our every need with generosity and grace. In Scripture, feasts often symbolize celebration, communion, and divine favor. From the Passover meal in Exodus to the Wedding Feast of the Lamb in Revelation, the Bible is replete with images of abundant tables prepared by God for His people. These feasts are not just about eating; they are about experiencing the fullness of God's blessings, His presence, and His unending love.

How does the image of a feast prepared by God deepen your understanding of His abundant provision and the joy of living in alignment with His will?

_____

_____

_____

_____

_____

Scriptural Reference:

- Psalm 23:5 (NIV): *"You prepare a table before me in the presence of my enemies. You anoint my head with oil; my cup overflows."*
- This verse emphasizes the idea of an overflowing cup, a symbol of abundance and blessings that exceed our needs and expectations.

2. Fulfillment of Desires

In what ways has the Provider fulfilled your deepest desires and needs, bringing you true satisfaction and joy?

_____

_____

_____

_____

_____

Scriptural Reference:

- Matthew 7:11 (NIV): *"If you, then, though you are evil, know how to give good gifts to your children, how much more will your Father in heaven give good gifts to those who ask him!"*
- This passage highlights the Provider's knowledge of our needs and the willingness to fulfill them generously.

3. Celebration of Life and Community

Feasts are often communal events, bringing people together in celebration. The table spread with delights symbolizes the joy of community and the shared blessings that come from being part of a larger spiritual family. It is a place of fellowship, where relationships are nurtured and strengthened. How can you embrace opportunities to celebrate life and build community with those around you?

_____

_____

_____

_____

_____

Scriptural Reference:

- Acts 2:46 (NIV): *"Every day they continued to meet together in the temple courts. They broke bread in their homes and ate together with glad and sincere hearts."*
- This description of the early Christian community underscores the importance of shared meals and fellowship as expressions of unity and joy.

Literal Significance of the Feast:
1. Physical Nourishment

How can you recognize and give thanks for the Creator's provision for your physical needs in your daily life?

_____
_____
_____
_____
_____

2. Diversity and Delight
How does the diversity of blessings in your life reflect the Creator's care for your unique needs and preferences?

_____
_____
_____
_____
_____

3. Gratitude and Enjoyment
Enjoying the feast is an act of gratitude. It is an opportunity to savor and appreciate the good things in life, recognizing them as gifts from the Provider. This enjoyment is not just about physical pleasure but also about cultivating a thankful heart and a sense of contentment.

Reflect on the times in your life when you have felt particularly blessed or provided for. Consider how these moments have been like a feast, offering you more than just physical sustenance but also joy, comfort, and a sense of being cared for.

_____
_____
_____
_____
_____

The table spread with all our favorite foods is a powerful symbol of the covenant of provision. It represents the abundance, generosity, and attention to our desires that the Provider offers. Both literally and symbolically, this feast is a reminder of the richness of life and the blessings available to us. As we partake in this feast, we are invited to celebrate, enjoy, and give thanks for the generosity and love of the Provider who ensures that we are never in lack.

~The Food I Need~

When we think of a table of provision, it is easy to focus on the delights and pleasures that satisfy our immediate desires. We envision a spread of our favorite foods, rich and abundant, catering to our cravings and bringing us joy in the moment. But the table of provision that God sets before us goes far beyond merely fulfilling our desires. It offers the sustenance we truly need—the nourishment that nurtures, strengthens, and supports our growth in every aspect of life: physically, spiritually, emotionally, and mentally.

At the most basic level, the table of provision offers us physical sustenance. Food is the foundation of life, providing the essential nutrients our bodies need to function, grow, and thrive. In Scripture, we see numerous examples of God providing physical nourishment to His people. From the manna in the wilderness that sustained the Israelites during their journey to the miraculous feeding of the 5,000, God's care for our physical needs is evident.

But, at the table of God, we're not just indulging in endless sweets and all our favorite comfort foods—the kind that, if left to our own devices, would have us popping waistbands, spiking glucose levels, and putting our dentists on speed dial. No, at this table, there's a wise and loving Father who knows how to balance out the menu. Sure, there are delights to savor, but He also dishes out generous portions of fruits and vegetables—those wholesome, nourishing foods that might not make us do a happy dance, but as Grandma always said, *"It might not taste good to you, but it's good for you."*

You see, at God's table, He's not just interested in feeding our cravings; He's nurturing our souls. He knows that life isn't all about the sweet stuff—sometimes we need the solid, nutrient-packed, stick-to-your-ribs kind of sustenance that helps us grow strong and healthy. And let's be honest, if it were up to us, we'd probably load up on dessert and skip the greens, but thankfully, God's got the perfect recipe for what we really need.

So while we might not always jump for joy at the sight of what's on our spiritual plate, we must trust that it's exactly what we need. That side of patience? It's just like spinach—maybe not our first pick, but it builds resilience. That helping of humility? It's like those Brussels sprouts—an acquired taste, but once we get it, we realize how it transforms our character.

And here's the kicker: as we learn to appreciate these dishes, we discover that they're not only good for us—they start to taste pretty darn good, too. Just like that moment when you realize roasted broccoli with a bit of garlic is actually delicious, or when you find yourself craving the crunch of a crisp apple. God knows how to turn the things we need into the things we start to love.

So, while we might come to the table expecting an all-you-can-eat buffet of our favorites, what we actually get is far better. We're served a balanced meal that feeds our bodies, minds, and spirits—carefully crafted by a Father who knows exactly what we need to thrive. And if we stick around long enough, we'll find that this divine menu doesn't just satisfy—it leaves us truly fulfilled, craving more of what's good for us.

However, this physical sustenance is more than just about survival. It is about God's abundant provision, His desire to not only meet our needs but to bless us with good things. As Psalm 104:14-15 beautifully illustrates, God provides food that not only sustains but also brings joy: *"He makes grass grow for the cattle, and plants for people to cultivate— bringing forth food from the earth: wine that gladdens human hearts, oil to make their faces shine, and bread that sustains their hearts."*

In providing this physical sustenance, God invites us to enjoy the goodness of His creation, to receive with gratitude the gifts He has given us, and to recognize that every meal, every bite, is a reflection of His care and love for us.

But the table of provision is not limited to physical sustenance. It also offers the spiritual nourishment that is essential for our souls. Just as our bodies need food to survive, our spirits need the nourishment that comes from a deep, ongoing relationship with God. Jesus Himself said, *"I am the bread of life. Whoever comes to me will never go hungry, and whoever believes in me will never be thirsty"* (John 6:35). This statement points to a spiritual reality: true sustenance comes from feeding on the Word of God, on His presence, and on His truth.

The table of provision offers us the opportunity to partake in this spiritual nourishment. Through prayer, meditation on Scripture, worship, and communion with God, we receive the sustenance that strengthens our faith, deepens our understanding, and fills our hearts with peace and joy. This spiritual food is not just about gaining knowledge; it is about experiencing the fullness of life that comes from being in right relationship with our Creator. It is about receiving the strength and grace we need to navigate the challenges of life, to grow in holiness, and to fulfill the purpose God has for us.

The table of provision also offers emotional sustenance. Life is filled with moments of joy, but it is also marked by times of sorrow, pain, and uncertainty. In these moments, we need more than just physical or spiritual nourishment; we need emotional support, comfort, and healing. The table of provision is a place where we can find this emotional sustenance.

God, in His compassion, invites us to bring our burdens to Him, to lay down our anxieties, fears, and wounds at His feet. In return, He offers us His comfort, His peace, and His healing touch. As Psalm 23:5-6 says, *"You prepare a table before me in the presence of my enemies. You anoint my head with oil; my cup overflows. Surely your goodness and love will follow me all the days of my life, and I will dwell in the house of the Lord forever."* The imagery of anointing and overflowing cups speaks to the abundance of God's emotional provision—He does not just meet our needs; He lavishes His love and care upon us, bringing healing to our brokenness and peace to our troubled hearts.

Finally, the table of provision offers us mental sustenance—the wisdom, understanding, and discernment we need to navigate the complexities of life. In a world filled with information overload, conflicting messages, and difficult decisions, we need more than just knowledge; we need the ability to think clearly, to discern truth from falsehood, and to make wise choices.

God's provision extends to our minds, offering us the wisdom that comes from His Word and His Spirit. James 1:5 tells us, *"If any of you lacks wisdom, you should ask God, who gives generously to all without finding fault, and it will be given to you."* This promise assures us that God is willing to provide the mental sustenance we need—whether it is clarity in decision-making, understanding in difficult situations, or the ability to think creatively and strategically.

At the table of provision, we are invited to feast on God's wisdom, to meditate on His truths, and to allow our minds to be renewed and transformed by His Spirit. This mental sustenance is crucial for our growth and development, enabling us to live lives that are not only successful but also aligned with God's will and purpose.

The table of provision that God spreads before us is a place of abundance, offering more than just the fulfillment of our desires. It is a source of sustenance that nurtures every aspect of our being—physically, spiritually, emotionally, and mentally. At this table, we find the nourishment we truly need, the sustenance that supports our growth, strengthens our faith, heals our wounds, and guides our decisions.

As we come to this table, let us do so with open hearts and minds, ready to receive the fullness of God's provision. Let us recognize that His care for us extends to every part of our lives, and that He is faithful to provide for us in ways that are far beyond what we could ask or imagine. The table is spread, and the feast of the Lord is going on—come, and be filled with the abundance that only God can offer.

The Balance Between Desires and Necessities

1. Understanding Needs vs. Wants

How can you focus on fulfilling your true needs before wants, trusting in the table of provision to bring balance, health, and growth into your life?

_____

_____

_____

_____

_____

Scriptural Reference:

- Philippians 4:19 (NIV): *"And my God will meet all your needs according to the riches of his glory in Christ Jesus."*

- This verse underscores the promise that our needs will be met, reflecting the Creator's understanding of what is truly essential for us.

2. The Role of Needs in Growth

Needs are not just about survival; they also play a crucial role in our growth and development. Just as proper nutrition is essential for physical health, spiritual, emotional, and mental nourishment are vital for our overall well-being. The table of provision includes everything we need to grow in these areas.

3. Recognizing and Accepting Necessary Provisions

Sometimes, what we need may not align with what we desire. Recognizing and accepting necessary provisions requires humility and trust. It involves understanding that the Provider knows what is best for us, even when it is not immediately apparent.

Reflect on a time when you received something you needed, but it wasn't what you initially wanted. How did this provision benefit you in the long run?

Stories of Divine Provision.

_____
_____
_____
_____

(Manna in the Wilderness)
A classic example of divine provision is the story of manna provided to the Israelites in the wilderness. This daily provision of food met their physical needs during a time of scarcity, teaching them reliance on divine sustenance.

Scriptural Reference:

- Exodus 16:4 (NIV): *"Then the Lord said to Moses, 'I will rain down bread from heaven for you. The people are to go out each day and gather enough for that day.'"*
- This story illustrates how the Creator provides precisely what is needed, even in the most challenging circumstances.
- Elijah and the Widow at Zarephath
  Another story of divine provision involves the prophet Elijah and a widow during a famine. Despite having only a small amount of flour and oil, the widow's resources were miraculously replenished, providing for both her family and Elijah.

Scriptural Reference:

- 1 Kings 17:14 (NIV): *"For this is what the Lord, the God of Israel, says: 'The jar of flour will not be used up and the jug of oil will not run dry until the day the Lord sends rain on the land.'"*

- This account highlights the miraculous provision of needs in times of desperation and the faith required to trust in such provision.
- Modern Testimonies
  In contemporary times, many people share stories of unexpected provision, whether it's financial support, emotional comfort, or spiritual guidance. These testimonies often involve situations where a critical need was met in a surprising and timely manner, reinforcing the belief in a caring and attentive Provider.

> Consider a time in your life when you experienced what you needed, even if it wasn't what you asked for. How did this provision help you grow or change?
>
> _____
> _____
> _____
> _____
> _____

"The Food I Need" emphasizes the importance of recognizing and appreciating the essentials provided to us. These provisions not only fulfill our immediate needs but also support our overall growth and well-being. By balancing our desires with our necessities and trusting in the Provider's wisdom, we can navigate life's challenges with assurance and gratitude. Stories of divine provision, both ancient and modern, remind us of the constant care and support available to us, encouraging us to trust in the sustaining power of the covenant.

~If Meat Offends You: Recognizing Dietary Restrictions~

Imagine this: you walk into a grand banquet, a feast that looks like something out of a foodie's wildest dreams. There's a table stretching as far as the eye can see, loaded with every type of dish imaginable. I'm talking collard greens, candied yams, and the kind of comfort food that warms your soul (all of my favorites). But wait—what's that over there? Casu Marzu (aka Maggot Cheese), Hákarl (yep, that's fermented shark),

Medama (yes, those are tuna eyeballs), and Pidan (century eggs that have aged like milk left out in the desert sun). One whiff of those delicacies, and suddenly, my appetite has plummeted.

Welcome to the "Taste of the World" event that I had the privilege of experiencing, where the menu is as diverse as the guests. It's a vivid reminder that what's on your neighbor's plate might be wildly different from what's on yours. But that's the beauty of it, right? It's the challenge—and the joy—of living in a world where everyone's tastes and needs are as unique as they are.

This, my friends, is the table of provision—a place where differences aren't just tolerated, they're celebrated. Here, everyone is welcome, and every dish, no matter how unusual, has a place. In a world filled with dietary restrictions, ethical choices, and personal preferences, this table isn't just a nice idea; it's absolutely essential.

At this table, inclusivity isn't the side dish—it's the main course. Whether you're all about that plant-based life, strictly gluten-free, keeping it kosher, or carb-loading like there's no tomorrow, there's something here with your name on it. The table of provision understands that everyone's got their own thing going on, and it meets those needs with an open heart and an open menu.

Let's be honest: when it comes to food, one size definitely doesn't fit all. Some of us are steering clear of gluten, others are dodging dairy like it's their ex, and a few wouldn't touch meat with a ten-foot fork. Then there are those who follow specific dietary laws, like kosher or halal, and others who choose plant-based diets because they care about the planet or animals. Whatever your reason, the table of provision isn't just accommodating these differences—it's embracing them like a long-lost friend.

This is what the table of provision is all about—creating a space where everyone's needs and preferences are honored. It's a reminder that in a truly inclusive environment, no one has to feel like they're "difficult" or "different." Instead, they're just one of many guests at a table where diversity is the spice of life.

Let's dive deeper. The table of provision is rooted in the covenant of provision—a divine agreement that's about way more than just food. It's about respecting and honoring the individuality that each person brings to the table. This covenant recognizes that our dietary choices aren't just random preferences; they're often deeply tied to who we are, our values, our beliefs, and our well-being.

For some, what they eat is directly linked to their faith. For others, it's a matter of health, making sure they can live their best life. And for others, it's about making ethical choices that align with their beliefs about the world. The covenant of provision makes room for all of these perspectives, ensuring that no one is left out or made to feel less than.

So, why does inclusivity matter so much at the table? Because the table isn't just a place where we eat; it's where we build relationships, share stories, and create community. When everyone's needs and preferences are respected, it sends a powerful message: You belong here. You matter. Your choices are important.

Inclusivity at the table also fosters a sense of unity. It brings people together who might otherwise be divided by their differences. When we take the time to honor each person's dietary needs and preferences, we're doing more than just feeding them—we're showing them that they are seen, heard, and loved. And in doing so, we create a table that's not just full of food, but full of life, connection, and joy.

So, what's the takeaway? The table of provision is a place where everyone is welcome, no matter their dietary needs or preferences. It's a table that celebrates diversity and inclusivity, offering something for everyone and ensuring that each person feels respected and valued. Whether you're coming for the food, the company, or both, you can be sure that there's a place for you at this table.

In a world that often feels divided, the table of provision is a beautiful reminder of what can happen when we come together with open hearts and open minds. It's a place where we can celebrate our differences, honor each other's choices, and enjoy the incredible abundance that comes from inclusivity. So, pull up a chair, dig in, and enjoy the feast—because at this table, everyone is welcome, and everyone is fed.

Inclusivity in Provision

1. Respecting Dietary Needs and Preferences

"How can I embrace God's covenant of provision in a way that honors and respects the diverse needs and choices of those around me?"

_____
_____
_____
_____
_____

Scriptural Reference:

- Romans 14:2-3 (NIV): *"One person's faith allows them to eat anything, but another, whose faith is weak, eats only vegetables. The one who eats everything must not treat with contempt the one who does not, and the one who does not eat everything must not judge the one who does, for God has accepted them."*

- This passage highlights the importance of accepting and respecting different dietary choices within a community of faith.

2. The Role of Compassion and Understanding

How can you show compassion and understanding at the table by honoring others' dietary needs, fostering a sense of belonging and reflecting the Creator's care for all?

_____
_____
_____
_____
_____

3. Practical Accommodations

How can you practice thoughtful and inclusive accommodations for dietary restrictions in your community to ensure that everyone can enjoy the shared bounty of the table without discomfort or exclusion?

_____
_____
_____
_____
_____

Ethical and Religious Considerations

1. Religious Dietary Laws

How do religious dietary laws and practices enrich your understanding of spirituality and culture, and how can you honor these traditions in your own life and community?

_____
_____
_____
_____
_____

Scriptural Reference:

- Leviticus 11:46-47 (NIV): *"These are the regulations concerning animals, birds, every living thing that moves about in the water and every creature that moves along the ground. You must distinguish between the unclean and the clean, between living creatures that may be eaten and those that may not be eaten."*

- This reference illustrates the importance of dietary laws in religious practice and how they are integrated into daily life.

2. Ethical and Health Considerations

How can understanding the ethical and health considerations behind dietary choices deepen your respect for diverse lifestyles and foster a more inclusive environment within your community?

_____
_____

_____

_____

_____

3. The Importance of Dialogue and Respect
How does engaging in open dialogue about dietary restrictions and preferences foster a culture of respect and empathy in your community, ensuring that everyone feels valued and included?

_____

_____

_____

_____

The table of provision is a powerful symbol of inclusivity and respect. By accommodating various dietary restrictions and preferences, it reflects the covenant's commitment to meeting the needs of all individuals. This inclusivity extends beyond mere food preferences to embody a broader principle of respect for diversity in all its forms. In a world with diverse dietary practices, the covenant encourages us to be compassionate and considerate, ensuring that everyone has a place at the table and can enjoy the feast provided. This respect for individual choices not only honors the unique needs of each person but also strengthens the bonds of community and shared fellowship.

Furthermore, the table of provision becomes a tangible expression of God's hospitality and grace, mirroring His desire for unity amidst diversity. Just as God welcomes all to His table without regard for status, background, or identity, we too are called to extend that same spirit of welcome and inclusion in our communities. This inclusive approach fosters an environment where differences are not merely tolerated but celebrated as part of the rich tapestry of God's creation. When we create space at the table for every person—acknowledging their unique perspectives, experiences, and needs—we reflect the heart of the covenantal promise: that God's love and provision are abundant and available to all. In this way, the table becomes more than just a place to eat; it transforms into a sacred space of belonging, reconciliation, and shared purpose, where the fullness of God's kingdom is glimpsed here on earth as we engage in the important work of tearing down the walls of tribalism that have created so much animus and strife in our world; bruising our collective humanity.

~Changing from Living to Eat to Eating to Live~

I once heard someone say, *"Eat food as your medicine, or you'll end up eating medicine as your food."* In today's fast-paced world, where convenience often trumps quality, we need to be more mindful of what we put on our plates. Let's be real—processed food is doing more harm than good. We've all indulged in that extra slice of pizza, the second helping of dessert, or that massive bowl of ice cream after a tough day. Food has become a source of comfort, celebration, and even a way to cope with stress. But what if we turned that idea on its head? Instead of living to eat, what if we started eating to live?

Imagine treating food not just as something to satisfy cravings but as fuel for a healthier, longer life. It's about choosing more from the earth and less from the box—embracing the idea that what we eat can be our greatest medicine. By flipping the script and making conscious choices, we can nourish our bodies in a way that keeps us thriving, not just surviving. So, let's start eating with intention, choosing foods that support our well-being and help us live our best lives. After all, it's easier to enjoy life when we're not constantly battling the consequences of poor food choices.

The covenant invites us to make this transformative shift in perspective—from living to eat, where food becomes the center of our existence, to eating to live, where food serves its true purpose: nourishing our bodies, fueling our lives, and enhancing our well-being. This change isn't about deprivation or denying ourselves the pleasures of good food. Instead, it's about embracing moderation over excess and appreciating the true value of sustenance. By adopting this mindset, we can cultivate a more mindful and balanced approach to both eating and living. And let's be real—it's a lot easier to enjoy that piece of cake when you know you're treating your body with the respect it deserves.

We've all been at the buffet where the plates are practically groaning under the weight of mashed potatoes, lasagna, and a little bit of salad—because, you know, balance. It's fun in the moment, but afterward, you might be left with that all-too-familiar feeling: "Why did I do this to myself?" That's where the shift from living to eat to eating to live comes in.

When we embrace eating to live, our plates might start to look a little different. Instead of piling on the food, we start thinking about what we're putting on our plates and why. Are we eating because we're hungry, or because we're bored? Are we choosing foods that will fuel our bodies and give us energy, or are we just going for what looks good in the moment? This shift doesn't mean we have to say goodbye to our favorite foods—far from it! It's about enjoying those foods in a way that supports our overall health and well-being.

Imagine savoring each bite, knowing that you're nourishing your body with what it truly needs. You'll start to notice the difference—not just in how you feel physically, but also in your relationship with food. Eating becomes an act of self-care, not self-indulgence. It's about quality over quantity, and about making choices that align with your values and your goals for a healthy, happy life.

Let's talk moderation—because, let's face it, life without chocolate cake is no life at all. But life with chocolate cake at every meal? Well, that's a recipe for disaster (and probably a stomachache). The key to eating to live is finding that sweet spot between deprivation and overindulgence.

Moderation doesn't mean saying no to the foods you love; it means saying yes to them in a way that fits into a balanced, healthy lifestyle. It's about enjoying your favorite treats without going overboard, and about making choices that feel good both in the moment and in the long run. When we eat to live, we're more mindful of our portions, more intentional about our choices, and more in tune with our bodies' signals. And guess what? That makes every meal more satisfying.

By embracing moderation, we free ourselves from the cycle of guilt and regret that often comes with overeating. We learn to enjoy our food without overindulging, to savor the flavors without feeling stuffed, and to appreciate the role that food plays in our lives without letting it take center stage.

Food is amazing—it's delicious, it's comforting, and it's a big part of our social lives. But at its core, food is fuel. It's what powers our bodies, keeps us healthy, and gives us the energy to do all the things we love. When we shift from living to eat to eating to live, we start to see food for what it really is: sustenance that supports us in living our best lives.

This mindset encourages us to choose foods that nourish our bodies, rather than just satisfy our cravings. It helps us to be more mindful about what we eat, to listen to our bodies' needs, and to make choices that support our health and well-being. And here's the best part: when we treat food as fuel, we actually end up enjoying it more. We're not just eating out of habit or boredom—we're eating with intention, and that makes every bite more meaningful.

"You are what you eat, so don't be fast, cheap, easy, or fake." This statement reminds us that the food we choose to consume directly reflects how we treat and value ourselves. When we opt for fast, cheap, easy, or fake foods, we're often compromising our health for convenience or momentary satisfaction. Just as a house built on a weak foundation won't stand strong, a body fueled by low-quality food won't thrive. Instead, we should aim to nourish ourselves with whole, real foods that provide genuine nutrients and lasting energy. Choosing foods that are rich in quality, natural, and thoughtfully prepared is an investment in our well-being, reflecting a commitment to self-care and respect. When we take the time to eat well, we're saying to ourselves and the world that we deserve the best—not just the easiest or most convenient option. So, let's strive to fill our bodies with food that is as authentic and vibrant as the life we wish to lead.

The Shift in Perspective

1. Understanding 'Living to Eat'

The phrase "living to eat" refers to a lifestyle focused on indulging in food for pleasure, often leading to excess and an unhealthy relationship with eating. This approach can result in overeating, neglecting nutritional needs, and a lack of mindfulness regarding the impact of food choices on overall health and well-being.

2. Embracing 'Eating to Live'

Conversely, "eating to live" means prioritizing nourishment and health over mere indulgence. This perspective focuses on eating to support life, health, and vitality. It involves making conscious choices about what, when, and how much to eat, with an emphasis on consuming nutrient-rich foods that sustain and energize the body.

Scriptural Reference:

- 1 Corinthians 6:19-20 (NIV): *"Do you not know that your bodies are temples of the Holy Spirit, who is in you, whom you have received from God? You are not your own; you were bought at a price. Therefore honor God with your bodies."*
- This passage highlights the importance of respecting and caring for our bodies, which includes making healthy and mindful choices about what we consume.

Mindful Eating

1. What is Mindful Eating?

Mindful eating is the practice of paying full attention to the experience of eating and drinking, both inside and outside the body. It involves noticing the colors, smells, textures, flavors, temperatures, and even the sounds (crunch!) of our food. Mindful eating also means being aware of the hunger and satiety signals from our body, recognizing the difference between physical hunger and emotional hunger. When is the last time you practiced mindful eating and why do you not do it more?

_____

_____

_____

_____

_____

2. Benefits of Mindful Eating

- Improved Digestion: Eating slowly and savoring food can aid digestion and improve the body's ability to absorb nutrients.

- Better Weight Management: Being mindful of portion sizes and hunger cues can prevent overeating and promote a healthy weight.

- Enhanced Enjoyment: Taking time to appreciate the flavors and textures of food can enhance the overall eating experience.

- Emotional Well-being: Mindful eating can help identify emotional triggers for eating, leading to healthier coping strategies.

_____
_____
_____
_____
_____

3. Practical Steps for Mindful Eating

Eat without Distractions: Avoid watching TV, using a phone, or working while eating. Focus solely on your meal.

- Chew Thoroughly: Chew each bite well to savor the flavors and aid digestion.

- Listen to Your Body: Pay attention to your body's hunger and fullness cues. Eat when you're hungry and stop when you're satisfied.

- Appreciate Your Food: Take a moment to appreciate where your food came from and the effort that went into preparing it.

_____
_____
_____
_____
_____

Living a Balanced Life

1. The Role of Nutrition in Well-being

How does recognizing the role of nutrition in your well-being encourage you to make mindful choices about your diet that support your physical health, mental clarity, and emotional stability?

_____
_____
_____
_____

2. The Spiritual Aspect of Eating

How can approaching the act of eating as a spiritual gift and practicing mindfulness and gratitude enhance your appreciation for the interconnectedness of life and the effort behind your sustenance?

_____
_____
_____
_____

3. Moderation and Self-control

How can practicing moderation and self-control in your daily choices help you align with your values and health goals while promoting a balanced approach to life?

_____
_____
_____
_____

Scriptural Reference:

- Proverbs 25:16 (NIV): *"If you find honey, eat just enough—too much of it, and you will vomit."*
- This proverb underscores the importance of moderation, even in consuming good things.

Changing from "living to eat" to "eating to live" is a profound shift that encourages us to view food as a source of nourishment rather than mere indulgence. This perspective fosters a healthier relationship with food, emphasizing the importance of moderation, mindful eating, and appreciation for the sustenance we receive. By adopting these principles, we can support our overall well-being and honor the gift of life, nurturing our bodies, minds, and spirits in harmony. The covenant guides us towards a balanced and fulfilling life, where we are mindful of our choices and grateful for the provisions we receive.

~*Everyone at The Table is Not Hungry*~

The late Adrian Rogers once shared a story that perfectly captures the essence of discontentment. A woman, eager to satisfy her perpetually complaining husband, asked him one morning what he wanted for breakfast. *"I want two eggs,"* he replied. *"One scrambled and one fried."* She obliged, serving him exactly what he asked for: one scrambled egg and one fried egg. But when she placed the plate before him, he frowned. Confused, she asked what was wrong. His response was as predictable as it was frustrating: *"You scrambled the wrong one."* Had his wife been some of the women I know, he definitely would've been wearing those eggs.

Dr. Rogers used this story to highlight a profound truth—people like this man aren't truly hungry. They aren't at the table to be nourished or satisfied; they're there to find fault, to criticize, and to complain. These are the people who, as Louie Giglio warns in his book, *"Don't Give the Enemy a Seat at Your Table,"* come with the wrong motives. They aren't seeking the sustenance that gives life; they're simply looking for something to pick apart, to confirm their preconceived dissatisfaction. We've all encountered these individuals in relationship: in church on our jobs etc.

Jesus addressed this mindset directly when He said, *"Do not work for food that spoils, but for food that endures to eternal life, which the Son of Man will give you. For on him God the Father has placed his seal of approval."* Yet even then, those listening missed the point. They asked Him, *"What must we do to do the works God requires?"* And when Jesus responded, *"The work of God is this: to believe in the one he has sent,"* they continued to press, demanding a sign, questioning, *"What sign then will you give that we may see it and believe you? What will you do? Our ancestors ate the manna in the wilderness; as it is written: 'He gave them bread from heaven to eat'"* (John 6:27-32).

Jesus replied with piercing clarity, *"Very truly I tell you, it is not Moses who has given you the bread from heaven, but it is my Father who gives you the true bread from heaven. For the bread of God is the bread that comes down from heaven and gives life to the world"* (John 6:32, 33).

The lesson here is clear: Not everyone who comes to the table is hungry for what truly matters. Many are present not because they seek the Bread of Life, but because they are drawn by what they think they can get from the table—be it comfort, status, or the mere satisfaction of finding fault. They are not committed to the nourishment that sustains; they are committed only to their own superficial desires.

We would do well to recognize that everyone at the table is not there for the right reasons. Some are like the husband who finds fault no matter what is placed before him—never truly hungry, never truly satisfied. They come to the table with an appetite for criticism, not communion. Their presence is not a reflection of their hunger for righteousness but of their attachment to the distractions and distortions that spoil and fade.

If we were to start breaking some plates—if we were to challenge these false appetites and remove the distractions—we might witness something revealing. Those who are not truly hungry, who are not there for the bread that gives life, would likely leave. They were never there for the meal; they were there to feed something else entirely.

This is a sobering reminder to examine our own motives when we approach the table of God's provision. Are we truly hungry for the bread of life, for the sustenance that only He can provide? Or are we merely seeking to satisfy lesser desires, critiquing what is offered rather than receiving it with gratitude?

The table of God's provision is not just a place to receive; it's a place to be transformed. But that transformation only happens when we come with the right hunger, with an openness to be filled with what truly satisfies. If our hearts are set on the wrong things, if we're more interested in what we can get than in what we are being given, we will miss the true nourishment that is offered. We must come to the table with a hunger for righteousness, a thirst for the living water, and a desire to be filled with the bread that gives life to the world. Only then will we find that we are truly satisfied, never to hunger or thirst again.

In his book, Louie Giglio's makes a keen observation, *"When you allow the enemy a seat at your table, you are allowing him to influence your thoughts, your emotions, your actions, and ultimately your life."* This serves as a poignant reminder that our mental and spiritual spaces are sacred. The "table" is a metaphor for the place where we engage in deep fellowship, reflection, and decision-making, a space meant to be filled with God's truth, love, and guidance. Yet, too often, we unknowingly or carelessly allow negative influences, deceptive voices, and destructive forces a seat at this sacred table. When we do this, we give them access to our most intimate thoughts, which then cascade into our emotions, decisions, and ultimately, the course of our lives.

This concept challenges us to guard our tables — to be vigilant about who or what we allow to have influence over our minds. It reminds us that not everyone or everything deserves a seat, as some influences are toxic and do not come to nurture but to devour. This is where the importance of discernment comes into play, not only in spiritual battles but also in our everyday interactions and relationships.

It has been my strong contention that before inviting others to the table — whether in the literal sense or as a metaphor for inviting them into our inner circle, our thoughts, or our trust — we must first assess what they have an appetite for. Not everyone who approaches our table comes with good intentions. Some are "cannibals" in the figurative sense: they come to take, to consume, and to feed off what you have without offering anything nourishing in return. They are driven by greed, envy, or personal gain. Such individuals have done a cold appraisal of your value, not to celebrate or uplift you, but to see what they can extract for themselves.

To extend this metaphor further, some people approach us not with an appetite for genuine connection, mutual growth, or shared purpose, but with a predatory mindset. They see your gifts, your peace, your joy, and your purpose as something to exploit. They've appraised your worth in terms of what they can gain, rather than how they can add value to your life or how you can build something greater together. It's as if they've already sized up your "head"—not to honor it, but to see how they might use it to their advantage.

This is why discernment is critical in both our spiritual lives and our daily relationships. When Jesus dined with sinners and tax collectors, He did so not out of naivety, but with clear purpose and divine wisdom. He knew their hearts, their intentions, and, more importantly, His mission. Likewise, we must exercise wisdom in whom we invite to our table. Not every conversation is worth having. Not every influence deserves a voice. Some come to sow doubt, to distract, to divide, or to destroy. And some come with an agenda that is entirely self-serving, driven by a spirit that is not of God but of the enemy.

So, how do we guard our tables? It starts with being deeply rooted in God's truth. When our foundation is strong, when we know the Shepherd's voice clearly, we can more easily recognize when a stranger or an intruder tries to speak lies into our lives. It also involves surrounding ourselves with those who reflect the love, grace, and truth of God—those who uplift, encourage, and challenge us in the right ways.

We need to assess the "appetites" of those around us. Do they hunger for righteousness, justice, and love, or do they crave chaos, conflict, and control? Are they here to build with you or to break you down? Not every person who smiles at you is a friend, and not every invitation to fellowship is worth accepting.

Ultimately, we must take ownership of our tables. Just as you wouldn't allow a thief or a destroyer into your home, you shouldn't allow destructive influences into your mind and heart. Guard your table with prayer, with wisdom, and with the constant awareness that not everyone deserves a seat. When we do this, we create space for God to fill us with His peace, His purpose, and His power, ensuring that our tables remain places of life, not battlegrounds for the enemy.

~In the Presence of My Enemies~

There's something deeply comforting about the promise that God will prepare a table for us in the presence of our enemies. It's like a divine declaration that says, "You've been wronged, but don't worry—I've got your back." Particularly when we've been hurt or deprived by others, this promise can feel like sweet vindication. Imagine sitting down to a feast, lovingly prepared by God Himself, right in front of those who sought to harm you. It's a powerful image—one that speaks to God's justice, provision, and unwavering faithfulness.

But as satisfying as that picture might be, there's a deeper truth here that goes beyond getting even. Sure, it's tempting to think of this as God's way of saying, "Watch how I bless you in front of those who tried to tear you down," but the real point of this promise is far more profound. It's not about us getting revenge or rubbing our enemies' noses in our blessings—it's about God getting the glory.

You see, when God sets that table for us, it's a demonstration of His faithfulness, His power, and His commitment to keep His promises. It's about Him showing up in our lives in such a way that even those who have wronged us can't deny His presence and goodness. The table isn't just a place of provision; it's a stage where God's glory is put on full display. He's not just providing for us—He's making a statement to the world: "I am faithful, I am good, and I take care of my children even when you (the world) try to deprive them."

Now, here's where the rubber meets the road: we have to be careful that our motivation for staying close to God isn't just about wanting to see our enemies put in their place. As tempting as it might be, that's not what this promise is about. It's not about us sitting at the table with a smug grin, thinking, "Look who's got the last laugh now." No, it's about recognizing that the real victory is in God's glory, not in our personal satisfaction.

Think about it—when God provides for us in front of those who've hurt us, it's a reminder that His blessings aren't just about making us feel better. They're about showing the world who He is. And sometimes, the most powerful way He does that is by blessing us in such a way that it leaves our enemies speechless—not because we've triumphed over them, but because God's goodness is undeniable.

So, yes, take comfort in the fact that God will prepare a table for you in the presence of your enemies. But remember that the true purpose of that table is not about getting even—it's about giving God the glory. It's about trusting that His provision, His justice, and His love are enough, even when we've been wronged. And when we sit at that table, let's do so with a heart full of gratitude, knowing that it's not about what we've overcome, but about who God is and how He keeps His promises. Because in the end, it's not about our enemies at all—it's about the faithful, loving God who never fails to provide.

When God prepares a table for us in the presence of our enemies, it is more than just an act of divine hospitality or protection—it is an affirmation of our right to self-determination. The concept of self-determination, or Kujichagulia in Swahili, is central to the philosophy of Kwanzaa and speaks to the powerful, transformative act of defining, naming, creating, and speaking for ourselves. In a world where many forces seek to control, limit, or suppress our potential, claiming our own table and defining what is on the menu becomes a radical act of autonomy and resistance.

The idea of self-determination challenges the narrative that others must decide our fate, define our identity, or dictate our worth. It is a declaration that we will no longer accept being told who we are or what we deserve. But here's the irony: those who insist that we "take responsibility for ourselves" often have no intention of truly letting us do so. When we do step into our own power and agency—when we build our own tables and set our own agendas—they show up uninvited, not to support but to supervise, not to celebrate but to control.

There is a reason why, throughout history, systems of power have been uncomfortable with the self-determination of marginalized communities. It threatens the status quo. When a people realize they no longer need permission to define themselves or to create their own future, they undermine the very foundations of those systems that have long benefited from their oppression. The rhetoric of "handouts" and "personal responsibility" is often a smoke screen to maintain dominance. The truth is, those who control the current tables are more than happy to see us dependent, but they become very nervous when we start building tables of our own.

The reality is, the complaints about "handouts" aren't about generosity being drained; they are about control being lost. It's not that they want us to be without a table—they just want to make sure they still get to decide what's served, who sits where, and who has access. As long as they can dictate the terms of our lives, they remain comfortable. But when we begin to embrace Kujichagulia—when we decide for ourselves what success looks like, what values we hold, what communities we build—they are forced to reckon with the fact that their power is not absolute.

Self-determination means deciding what will nourish us spiritually, culturally, and materially. It means refusing to let anyone else dictate our menu, to tell us that we can only eat what they are willing to offer. We must reject the scraps and the leftovers, and instead, cultivate the strength, wisdom, and unity to build our own tables, stocked with the abundance that is rightfully ours. This is not just about physical or economic independence but about reclaiming our narrative, our stories, and our destiny.

In this context, God preparing a table in the presence of our enemies is a profound act of divine endorsement of our right to exist fully and freely. It is God saying, "You have a place, and that place is yours to define." The presence of enemies only makes the table more significant—it stands as a testament that no amount of opposition can invalidate the seat that God has prepared for us. But that also means we must take up the responsibility to sit at that table with boldness and clarity of purpose. We must not allow the opinions, fears, or manipulations of our enemies to dictate our agenda.

So, what does it mean to have our own table and our own menu? It means we choose to feed ourselves with the food of dignity, justice, and freedom. It means we are deliberate in cultivating spaces that nourish our minds, bodies, and souls. It means we are unapologetic about who sits at our table and who does not, understanding that our liberation is not up for negotiation.

To be determined to have our own table and set our own menu is not about being territorial, embracing rugged individualism, or relying solely on self to the extent that we see no need for others. Instead, it is about embracing the fullness of self-determination. It is declaring that, with God, we are co-authors of our destiny, possessing the wisdom to govern ourselves and rejecting any system that would force us to beg for a seat at a table never intended for us. It is a commitment to stewardship principles, serving at the table God establishes in our midst with responsibility and accountability.

Our ancestors, especially those who endured oppression and marginalization, understood this deeply. They recognized the power of self-determination, community-building, and self-definition. They knew that true freedom requires us to create, cultivate, and protect spaces where our identities, dreams, and goals are not subject to anyone else's approval. As we carry this legacy forward, let us commit to building our tables with intention, love, and purpose, ensuring that what we serve and how we serve it reflects our collective strength and resilience. Let us be clear: we will not wait for permission to live fully, and we certainly won't allow anyone else to decide what's on our menu. In choosing this path, we gain the power to dine in the presence of those who once sought to deny us.

~Never Eat Alone~

Keith Ferrazzi's book, *"Never Eat Alone,"* delves into the art of networking and offers practical strategies for harnessing the power of relationships to build a fulfilling career and life. Ferrazzi argues that success isn't just about what you know, but who you know and, more importantly, what you can create together. This idea of building through togetherness strikes a chord—though I must admit, the introvert in me still finds great solace in the quiet comfort of dining alone. Still, Ferrazzi's premise makes perfect sense: life is a collaborative endeavor, and the connections we make often pave the way to greater possibilities.

As the saying goes, *"Life is like a dinner table; it's better when shared."* This wisdom captures not just the joy of sharing meals with others but also the richness that comes from sharing our journeys, ideas, and dreams with those around us. After all, nobody ever remembers the best meal they ate alone—but they'll always remember the conversations, the laughter, and the bonds formed over a shared meal.

The Magic of Building Together:
Building together is where the magic happens. When we bring our unique skills, talents, and perspectives to the table and mix them with those of others, we create something far greater than what we could achieve alone. It's like a potluck dinner—everyone brings their best dish, and together, we end up with a feast that has a bit of everything. Alone, you might have had a sandwich, but together, you've got a five-course meal. And let's be honest, life is just tastier that way.

Take, for instance, the story of Apple's rise to prominence. Steve Jobs was undeniably a genius, but he wasn't a one-man show. Apple was built by a team of people who brought their unique strengths to the table—people like Steve Wozniak, who handled the technical wizardry, and Jony Ive, who brought the sleek, minimalist design that became Apple's hallmark. Together, they created a company that transformed technology and culture. Alone, they might have had great ideas; together, they had a revolution.

Togetherness as an Antidote to Isolation:
In an age where we are more digitally connected than ever, many of us are feeling more isolated and alone. But Ferrazzi's advice offers a counter-narrative: that meaningful success comes from authentic connections, not just digital likes or retweets. When we choose to build together, we find support, encouragement, and the opportunity to see things from new perspectives. We challenge each other, hold each other accountable, and celebrate each other's successes. In doing so, we create a community that isn't just about networking but about nurturing.

Iron Sharpens Iron: The Power of Collective Growth:
When we surround ourselves with the right people, we sharpen each other's ideas and expand our horizons. The old proverb says, "Iron sharpens iron, so one person sharpens another." When we build through togetherness, we are continually sharpening our skills, refining our thoughts, and pushing each other to grow. Alone, we might plateau; together, we can keep climbing higher.

Consider the power of peer mentorship or mastermind groups—small, committed circles of people who gather regularly to brainstorm, provide feedback, and offer support. These groups are not just networking opportunities; they are incubators for growth. Members of these groups often find that their ideas are enhanced, their confidence boosted, and their results multiplied by the collective wisdom and support of the group.

The Joy of Co-Creation:
There is something profoundly satisfying about co-creation—about rolling up your sleeves and getting into the creative trenches with someone else. When we build together, we share the load and the laughter, the late nights and the breakthroughs. We experience the joy of watching a project come to life, knowing that it was a team effort. It's like being in a band: sure, a solo act can be great, but there's nothing like the harmony of playing together, each person adding their unique flair to the music. When we get in the pocket together the sound is much more glorious than a single instrument.

Embracing the Awkwardness:
Now, for my fellow introverts who may feel overwhelmed by the idea of "never eating alone"—let's acknowledge the reality that, for some of us, networking doesn't always come naturally. It can feel a bit like speed dating for friendships, and we'd rather curl up with a good book than make small talk over lunch. But building together doesn't mean forcing yourself into situations that drain you. It's about finding your tribe—the people with whom conversations flow effortlessly, and collaboration feels energizing rather than exhausting. It's about quality over quantity, depth over superficiality.

So, let's embrace the awkwardness of reaching out, the vulnerability of saying, "I'd love to work with you," and the courage it takes to open up to others. Because on the other side of that awkwardness, there's potential—potential for friendships that inspire, partnerships that thrive, and communities that uplift. By stepping into this space of authenticity and openness, we create opportunities for genuine connection, where walls come down and true collaboration begins. It is in these moments of honesty and risk-taking that we find common ground and build bridges that span differences. In a world often marked by isolation and division, choosing to lean into the discomfort of forming new relationships can lead to transformative experiences that enrich our lives and broaden our horizons. When we dare to be vulnerable and take that first step toward connection, we invite a ripple effect of trust, creativity, and growth that not only benefits us but also has the power to impact those around us in profound and lasting ways.

Together, We Create Something Greater:
There's a popular saying, *"You're either at the table or on the menu."* While this adage may carry a bit of street-smart wisdom, it also reflects a troubling reality about how we've come to see the world—particularly in American culture. This phrase encapsulates a stark, binary mindset that reduces our choices to only two options: predator or prey, winner or loser. We find ourselves managing an untenable shark tank, where survival seems to depend on outmaneuvering and overpowering others. This mindset breeds a spirit of scarcity—an impoverished way of thinking that says, "If I'm to win, you must lose." But is this really the only way to live?

What if we rejected this zero-sum game and embraced a different paradigm—one where there's more than enough room for all of us? Where my success doesn't have to come at the expense of yours, and where collaboration, not competition, is the key to thriving? The truth is, there are enough resources—enough ideas, enough opportunities, enough love—for all of us to win, to eat, to grow, and to flourish. A mindset that focuses on abundance, rather than scarcity, creates a culture of generosity and growth rather than greed and division.

Togetherness isn't just a fluffy ideal; it's a powerful strategy for creating something far more meaningful and sustainable. When we come together, we lift each other up; we amplify each other's voices; we build something that is greater than the sum of its parts. We don't just achieve success; we create a legacy that is richer, deeper, and more impactful than anything we could accomplish alone. It's about recognizing that we are truly better together—that life, like a well-laid dinner table, is more nourishing, more fulfilling, and more joyful when shared.

So, let's change the narrative. Let's take a cue from thought leaders like Keith Ferrazzi, who reminds us that the most powerful connections are made when we set a bigger table. A table where there's room for everyone—where every person brings their own unique gifts, perspectives, and strengths to the feast. Imagine the incredible things we could build together, including the building up of one another. When we stop seeing each other as rivals and start seeing each other as partners in a greater mission, we begin to unlock a new level of potential and possibility.

Let's choose to build not in isolation but in community. Let's make the conscious decision to push back against the "eat or be eaten" mentality and instead embrace the mindset of "together, we rise." Let's commit to a new kind of table, one where everyone has a seat, and the only competition is to see who can serve the most generously. In doing so, we don't just create a table; we create a movement. And in that movement, we find the true meaning of wealth, success, and a life well-lived.

Chapter 3
Saying Grace

"God is great. God is good. Let us thank Him for our food. Amen!" Those simple words are etched into my memory, like a melody that plays before every meal, marking the start of something sacred. From the earliest moments of my childhood, this prayer was more than just a routine—it was a solemn ritual. My mom made sure of that. In our home, you didn't dare sneak a crumb before giving thanks; grace was non-negotiable. For her, it wasn't just a quick acknowledgment; it was a moment of reverence, a way to transform the ordinary act of eating into a sacred experience. The table, the food, and the prayer—they were inseparable, a trinity of sorts that made each meal an act of worship.

This tradition, rooted in my upbringing, is one that I've carried into my own family. My wife and I have passed it down to our sons (Not the exact same prayer), making it a cherished part of our daily routine. It's more than just a habit; it's become a kind of sacred tradition, a way of instilling in our boys a deep sense of gratitude and reverence. For Jackson, our oldest, saying grace is a serious responsibility. He loves leading the prayer, taking pride in the words he speaks before we eat. Jordan, on the other hand, is still learning the ropes. His hunger sometimes gets the better of him, and he'll sneak a bite before the prayer has even started. Jackson, ever the rule-keeper, is quick to correct him, often mid-bite, with a stern, *"You forgot to pray!"* And there's Jordan, sheepish and caught in the act, mumbling through a mouthful, *"Oh, sorry."*

It's a scene that repeats itself often at our dinner table, but it's more than just a playful sibling exchange. It's a constant reminder of how blessed we are, and it's teaching both boys some valuable life lessons. For Jackson, it's a lesson in grace itself. He's learning that while it's important to uphold tradition, it's equally important to show kindness and understanding. God's grace, after all, covers our missteps, so why shouldn't he extend that same grace to his brother?

For Jordan, the lesson is one of patience and gratitude. He's learning that his hunger, though real, doesn't need to control him. There's value in pausing, in taking a moment to recognize the abundance before him and to express thanks for it. The food isn't going anywhere, and by slowing down, he's beginning to understand the importance of acknowledging the Provider before diving into the provision.

These moments at the dinner table, filled with both laughter and learning, are shaping the boys in ways that go beyond simple manners. They're learning about discipline and grace, about the importance of gratitude and the joy that comes from recognizing blessings. They're understanding that the act of saying grace isn't just a box to check off before eating; it's a way of grounding ourselves in thankfulness, of connecting with each other and with something greater than ourselves.

As I watch Jackson and Jordan navigate these lessons, I'm reminded that these rituals we pass down are more than just traditions—they're foundational practices that shape our character and our understanding of the world. Saying grace is teaching our sons that life is filled with moments worth pausing for, worth acknowledging with gratitude. It's showing them that, even in the midst of everyday chaos, there's always time to recognize the blessings we've been given and to express our thanks.

In a world that often rushes from one thing to the next, these simple acts of pausing and giving thanks are more important than ever. They remind us to slow down, to be present, and to appreciate the abundance in our lives—whether that abundance is found in a meal shared with family, in the love and laughter that fills our home, or in the quiet moments of reflection and gratitude that ground us.

So, as we continue this tradition, I hope that Jackson and Jordan carry these lessons with them long after they leave our table. I hope they always remember to pause, to give thanks, and to recognize the grace that surrounds them. Because in those moments of gratitude, we're not just saying words—we're shaping hearts, building character, and connecting with the divine in the most ordinary of moments. And that, in itself, is a blessing worth celebrating every day.

~Praying for Daily Bread~

Praying for daily bread is a practice as ancient as it is enduring, a ritual that has woven itself into the fabric of countless cultures and faith traditions. It's a simple yet profound act that carries within it layers of meaning and significance. At its core, praying for daily bread is about recognizing and expressing gratitude for the basic sustenance that keeps us alive. But it's also much more than that—it's a humble acknowledgment of our deep dependence on the Provider, the One who ensures that our needs are met, day by day.

The phrase *"daily bread"* itself originates from the Lord's Prayer, a cornerstone of Christian practice, where Jesus teaches His followers to pray, *"Give us this day our daily bread."* This request is not just about asking for food; it's a symbolic expression of our trust in God's ongoing provision. In a world where self-sufficiency and independence are often prized, this prayer reminds us that, ultimately, we are not the masters of our own sustenance. Instead, we are dependent on the Creator who provides for us in ways both seen and unseen.

Saying grace before a meal is perhaps the most common way this prayerful tradition is kept alive in households around the world. Whether whispered quietly at a solitary breakfast or spoken aloud around a bustling dinner table, this moment of prayer serves as a powerful reminder of the blessings we receive each day. It's a pause—a brief but intentional break in the routine—to reflect on the source of our nourishment. In saying grace, we acknowledge that what is set before us is not to be taken for granted, but is a gift to be cherished.

Historically, the act of praying for daily bread has been a cornerstone of communal life. In agrarian societies, where food production was a daily struggle against the elements, this prayer was a lifeline, connecting people to a higher power amidst the uncertainty of the harvest. It was a prayer that held communities together, fostering a shared sense of dependence and humility. Even today, in our modern world where food is often abundant and easily accessible, this practice remains vital. It grounds us in the reality that all we have is not of our own making, but is provided by a source greater than ourselves.

The importance of this practice lies not just in the act of asking, but in the cultivation of gratitude and mindfulness. When we pray for daily bread, we're reminded to appreciate what we have—both the simple and the extraordinary. It shifts our focus from what we lack to what we've been given, fostering a mindset of thankfulness. This attitude of gratitude, in turn, has a ripple effect, influencing how we interact with others and how we view the world. It opens our eyes to the abundance around us, helping us to recognize and celebrate the small blessings that we might otherwise overlook.

Moreover, praying for daily bread invites us into a posture of mindfulness. In a fast-paced world where meals are often hurried and distractions abound, taking a moment to pray slows us down. It brings us into the present moment, encouraging us to savor not just the food, but the experience of eating, the company of others, and the connection to the divine. This mindfulness extends beyond the meal itself, influencing how we approach other areas of our lives with a greater sense of presence and awareness.

In this way, the simple act of praying for daily bread becomes a profound spiritual practice. It is a daily discipline that cultivates a heart of gratitude, a spirit of humility, and a mind attuned to the blessings of each moment. As we explore the history and importance of this practice, we begin to see how this small, everyday prayer has the power to transform not just our mealtime rituals, but our entire approach to life. It reminds us that we are part of something larger, something sacred, and that each meal, each day, is an opportunity to connect with the Provider who sustains us with love and generosity.

The History of Praying for Daily Bread
1. Biblical Origins
How does the biblical origin of the phrase "daily bread" in the Lord's Prayer deepen your understanding of reliance on God's provision for your daily needs?

_____

_____

_____

2. Broader Religious Context
How does understanding the practice of praying for sustenance across various religious traditions, such as the Jewish Birkat Hamazon, enrich your appreciation for the role of gratitude in recognizing God as the source of all nourishment?

3. Cultural Practices
Throughout history, cultures around the world have incorporated prayers or rituals expressing gratitude for food and sustenance. Whether through formal prayers, blessings, or simple expressions of thanks, these practices serve to recognize the effort and resources that provide nourishment. How were these types of prayers incorporated in your family?

The Importance of Praying for Daily Bread
1. Acknowledgment of Dependence
Praying for daily bread is an acknowledgment of our dependence on a higher power for our needs. It is a recognition that, despite our efforts, we are ultimately reliant on something greater than ourselves for provision. This practice fosters humility, reminding us of our interconnectedness with the Creator and the natural world. In what ways can I deepen my acknowledgment of dependence on God for daily provision,

fostering humility and a sense of connection with the Creator and creation?

_____
_____
_____
_____

2. Cultivating Gratitude

How does expressing gratitude through prayer before meals help cultivate a thankful heart and shift your focus from what you lack to recognizing all the blessings in your life?

_____
_____
_____
_____

3. Spiritual Nourishment

How does recognizing the need for daily spiritual nourishment alongside physical sustenance encourage you to seek spiritual growth and guidance regularly in your life?

_____
_____
_____
_____

Scriptural Reference:

- Matthew 6:11 (NIV): *"Give us today our daily bread."*
- This line from the Lord's Prayer emphasizes the daily nature of our dependence on God's provision, encouraging a continuous relationship with the divine.

Practical Application

1. Incorporating Prayer into Daily Life

To incorporate this practice into daily life, individuals can:

- Say a prayer or blessing before meals, thanking the Provider for the food and asking for continued provision.
- Reflect on the source of the food, including the efforts of farmers, workers, and the natural world.
- Consider the needs of others, praying for those who are without adequate food and resources.

_____

_____

_____

_____

_____

2. Extending Gratitude beyond Meals

How can you extend your practice of gratitude beyond mealtimes to enhance your overall well-being and deepen your spiritual practice through regular moments of reflection and thankfulness?

_____

_____

_____

_____

_____

Praying for daily bread is a profound practice that goes beyond the mere act of asking for food. It is a reminder of our dependence on the Provider for every blessing, a cultivation of gratitude, and an invitation to mindfulness. This practice encourages us to live with a greater awareness of the blessings we receive and to acknowledge the divine source of our sustenance. By incorporating prayer and gratitude into our daily lives, we can nurture a more profound connection with the Creator and the world around us, enriching both our spiritual and physical well-being.

~Giving Thanks for What He Has Done~

Let's face it—life isn't always a bed of roses. Sometimes it feels more like a bed of thorns, with the occasional rose thrown in just to keep things interesting. But here's the secret sauce for turning those prickly situations into moments of pure joy: gratitude. Yes, that simple, old-fashioned habit our grandmothers swore by can actually transform our heart, our perspective, and even our entire life. And the best part? It's free, easy to do, and doesn't require any fancy equipment—just a thankful heart and a willingness to see the good in every situation, even when it's hiding behind a cloud of chaos.

Gratitude is like a magical pair of glasses that makes everything in life look a little brighter, shinier, and more hopeful. When we start practicing gratitude, we begin to see the world differently. Suddenly, that annoying traffic jam becomes an opportunity to enjoy our favorite podcast, that stressful deadline at work becomes a chance to prove just how awesome we are under pressure, and even the rainiest of days becomes an excuse to cozy up with a good book and a cup of tea.

By giving thanks, we acknowledge the blessings we have received, and here's the kicker: we open ourselves up to experiencing even more. It's like the universe hears our gratitude and says, "Oh, you like that? Well, here's some more!" Gratitude has this amazing way of multiplying blessings, turning the ordinary into the extraordinary and the mundane into the magical.

But gratitude isn't just about us and our happy little bubble. It's also a powerful way to deepen our connection with others and with the Provider who makes all those blessings possible. When we express gratitude, we're sending out ripples of positivity that touch everyone around us. A simple "thank you" can brighten someone's day, strengthen a relationship, and create a sense of community and belonging.

And let's not forget the Provider—whether we call Him God, the Universe, or something else, expressing gratitude is like sending a cosmic thank-you note that strengthens our relationship with the

Source of all good things. It's a way of acknowledging that you're not in this alone, that there's a higher power looking out for you, guiding us, and providing for us. And when we take the time to say thanks, we're not just being polite—we're building a deeper, more meaningful connection with the very force that sustains us.

To really grasp the transformative power of gratitude, let's dive into some stories and reflections that might just inspire us to start our own gratitude practice—if we haven't already.

Consider the story of Jessica, a woman who, after losing her job, felt like her world was falling apart. She was angry, frustrated, and filled with self-doubt. But then, she decided to try something different: she started a gratitude journal. Every day, she wrote down three things she was thankful for, even on the days when it felt like there was nothing to be thankful for. At first, it was hard. But gradually, she noticed a shift. She began to see opportunities where she once saw obstacles. She reconnected with her passions, found a new job that was even better than the one she'd lost, and, most importantly, she regained her sense of joy and purpose. Gratitude didn't just change her perspective—it changed her life.

Or take Daren, a man who always seemed to be in a rush, barely noticing the world around him. One day, after reading about the benefits of gratitude, he decided to try a little experiment. Every time he felt annoyed or stressed, he paused, took a deep breath, and found something to be grateful for in that moment. Maybe it was the fact that he had a job that challenged him, or that his morning coffee was particularly delicious that day, or that his commute gave him a chance to listen to his favorite tunes. Over time, Tom found that he was less stressed, more patient, and, to his surprise, even more productive. Gratitude didn't just improve his mood—it improved his entire way of being.

The Transformative Power of Gratitude
1. Recognizing Abundance
How can practicing gratitude help you shift your focus from what you lack to recognizing the abundance in your life, fostering a

deeper appreciation for your possessions, relationships, and experiences?

_____
_____
_____
_____
_____

Scriptural Reference:

- 1 Thessalonians 5:18 (NIV): *"Give thanks in all circumstances; for this is God's will for you in Christ Jesus."*
- This verse encourages us to cultivate gratitude regardless of our circumstances, recognizing that every situation offers something to be thankful for.

2. Opening the Heart to Receive More

Expressing gratitude has the remarkable effect of opening our hearts to receive more blessings. Why do you think expressing gratitude opens our hearts? And in what ways can acknowledging what you have foster a mindset of abundance and optimism in your life?

_____
_____
_____
_____
_____

3. Enhancing Relationships

Gratitude strengthens our relationships with others. By expressing thanks for the kindness and support we receive, we reinforce bonds and build stronger connections. Gratitude also fosters empathy and compassion, helping us to see and appreciate the efforts and intentions of those around us. It encourages a mindset of recognizing the good in people and situations, which can transform our interactions from transactional to truly relational. When we practice gratitude consistently, we create a culture of appreciation that uplifts and encourages, making people feel valued and seen. This, in turn, cultivates a positive and supportive environment where trust can flourish and relationships can deepen, leading to a more connected and harmonious community.

Stories and Reflections on Gratitude
1. A Story of Gratitude in Adversity

In times of adversity, gratitude can be a powerful tool for resilience. One inspiring story is that of a family facing financial difficulties. Despite their challenges, they made a conscious effort to express gratitude for the small things they had—each other's support, the food on their table, and the kindness of friends and neighbors. This attitude not only helped them cope with their situation but also attracted unexpected blessings, such as job opportunities and financial assistance.

Reflect on a challenging time in your life and consider how gratitude might have helped you through it. What were the small blessings or moments of support that you appreciated?

_____
_____
_____
_____
_____

2. The Ripple Effect of Gratitude

Another reflection on gratitude involves its ripple effect. A simple act of gratitude, like thanking a colleague for their help, can inspire a chain of positive actions. One person's expression of thanks can lead to increased morale, stronger teamwork, and a more positive environment. This ripple effect shows that gratitude is not just beneficial for the individual but also for the community.

Reflection: Think about a time when someone's gratitude positively impacted you. How did it make you feel, and how did it influence your actions?

_____
_____
_____
_____

3. Gratitude in Everyday Life

Gratitude is not limited to extraordinary circumstances; it can be practiced in everyday life. For example, a person might keep a gratitude journal, jotting down three things they are thankful for each day. This simple practice can significantly shift one's perspective, making it easier to notice and appreciate the good in daily life.

Reflection: Consider starting a gratitude journal or setting aside a few minutes each day to reflect on what you are thankful for. How might this practice change your outlook?

_____
_____
_____
_____

Practical Steps to Cultivate Gratitude
1. Daily Gratitude Practice

How can you incorporate a daily gratitude practice into your routine, such as journaling, prayer, or reflection, to consistently acknowledge the good things in your life?

_____
_____
_____

_____

_____

2. Expressing Thanks

How can you make it a habit to express heartfelt gratitude to others, and what impact do you think this practice could have on both your life and theirs?

_____

_____

_____

_____

Giving thanks for what has been done for us is a powerful practice that can transform our hearts and lives. By focusing on gratitude, we acknowledge the abundance in our lives, open ourselves to more blessings, and strengthen our relationships with others. The stories and reflections shared here are meant to inspire and encourage a deeper practice of gratitude, helping us to appreciate the many gifts we receive daily. As we cultivate a thankful heart, we not only enrich our own lives but also contribute positively to the world around us, spreading joy, contentment, and kindness.

~A Reminder of How Blessed We Are~

Let's take a moment to talk about grace—no, not the kind you gracefully avoid when you're about to trip over your own feet (though we've all been there). We're talking about the kind of grace that gently nudges us and says, "Hey, slow down and take a look around. You're more blessed than you think." Grace is like that wise, calm friend who always knows just what to say to help you see the silver lining, even on the cloudiest of days. It's the little voice in your head that reminds you to count your blessings instead of your complaints.

Grace serves as a powerful reminder of the blessings we have, both big and small. It's the thing that helps us stop obsessing over what we don't have and start appreciating what we do. And let's be honest, when we start looking at life through the lens of grace, we realize that we've got it pretty good—like, "finding $20 in your winter coat pocket" kind of good.

Ever notice how easy it is to get stuck in a mindset of scarcity? We're constantly bombarded with messages that tell us we need more—more stuff, more success, more of whatever everyone else seems to have. It's like living in a perpetual state of "not enough." But here's where grace steps in like a superhero, cape and all, ready to save the day. Grace flips the script and shifts our focus from what's missing to what's already here. It's like putting on a pair of glasses that suddenly makes everything crystal clear: "Wait a minute—I have more than enough!"

When we embrace grace, we move from a mindset of scarcity to one of abundance. We start to see that our lives are filled with blessings, even if they don't always look the way we expected. Sure, maybe you don't have the latest gadget or a yacht parked in the marina, but you do have a cozy home, a warm meal, and people who care about you. And let's not forget about the little things—the perfect cup of coffee on a chilly morning, the sound of laughter echoing through your home, or that moment of peace when you finally kick off your shoes after a long day. Grace helps us see that these are the real treasures, the ones that make life rich and meaningful.

Here's the thing about blessings: they love to be noticed. They're like that plant in the corner of your living room that perks up when you finally remember to water it. When we take the time to recognize and celebrate our blessings, they seem to multiply. It's like the universe says, "Oh, you like that? Here, have some more!"

So, how do we start celebrating our blessings? It's easier than you might think. First, make it a habit to take stock of your day and notice the good things, no matter how small. Did you find a parking spot right in front of the store? Blessing. Did your friend send you a funny meme that made you laugh out loud? Double blessing. Did you manage to get through the day without spilling coffee on your shirt? Hallelujah, that's a blessing too!

Next, don't be shy about sharing your gratitude. Tell your loved ones how much you appreciate them. Post that beautiful sunset picture on social media and caption it with something like, "Feeling blessed to witness this today." When we share our blessings, we spread joy—and who doesn't need a little more of that?

Now, let's talk about contentment—a word that sometimes gets a bad rap in our go-go-go culture. Contentment doesn't mean settling for less or giving up on your dreams. It means finding peace and joy in the present moment, even as you work toward your goals. It's about realizing that life's little moments of happiness add up to something truly beautiful.

When grace helps us recognize our blessings, it naturally cultivates a heart full of contentment and joy. We stop chasing after every shiny thing and start appreciating the sparkle in what we already have. Contentment is like that warm blanket on a cold night—it wraps around you and makes everything feel just right.

And here's the best part: when your heart is full of contentment and joy, it's contagious. People around you start to notice that you're not just surviving—you're thriving. Your positive outlook becomes a beacon of light, guiding others to find their own grace-filled moments.

So, what's the takeaway? Grace is the key to unlocking a life rich with blessings. It's the gentle reminder that we're already blessed beyond measure, even when life gets a little chaotic. By embracing grace, we shift from a mindset of scarcity to one of abundance, celebrating the blessings in our lives and cultivating a heart full of contentment and joy.

In this fast-paced world, grace invites us to slow down, look around, and appreciate the beauty of the present moment. It encourages us to celebrate our blessings, no matter how small, and to share that joy with others. So, let's make grace a daily practice—let it remind us of how blessed we truly are, and inspire us to live each day with a heart full of gratitude, contentment, and joy. Because when we live a life enriched by grace, we find that we already have everything

Recognizing Our Blessings

1. The Shift from Scarcity to Abundance

In today's fast-paced world, it's easy to fall into a scarcity mindset, constantly focusing on what we lack or desire. How can shifting your focus from a scarcity mindset to an abundance mindset help you acknowledge and appreciate the blessings already present in your life?

_____

_____

_____

_____

_____

Scriptural Reference:

- Psalm 103:2 (NIV): *"Praise the Lord, my soul, and forget not all his benefits."*
- This verse encourages us to remember and be grateful for the many blessings we receive, urging us to count our blessings rather than our lacks.

2. The Power of Small Blessings

Often, we overlook the small, everyday blessings that enrich our lives. How can recognizing and appreciating the small, everyday blessings in your life cultivate a more mindful and grateful attitude?

_____

_____

_____

_____

_____

3. Gratitude for Challenges and Growth

How can recognizing the hidden blessings in challenges and hardships help you appreciate the growth and resilience that arise from adversity?

_____
_____
_____
_____

Celebrating Our Blessings
1. Practicing Gratitude Daily
One of the most effective ways to recognize and celebrate our blessings is through a daily gratitude practice. This can include:

- Gratitude Journaling: Writing down three things you are grateful for each day this week.
- Gratitude Meditation: Reflecting on your blessings during meditation or prayer.
- Sharing Gratitude: Expressing your gratitude to others, whether verbally or in writing.

_____
_____
_____
_____

2. Celebrating Milestones and Achievements
How can you take time to celebrate your achievements and milestones, recognizing the effort behind them and appreciating both the journey and the destination?

_____
_____
_____
_____

Reflecting on Blessings in Community
1. Sharing Stories of Gratitude

How can sharing stories of gratitude with others enhance your sense of blessing and joy, and strengthen your bonds within your family or community?

_____
_____
_____
_____

2. Acts of Kindness
How can you celebrate your blessings by paying them forward through acts of kindness, both big and small, to spread gratitude and abundance in your community?

_____
_____
_____
_____

3. Rituals and Traditions
How can you incorporate rituals and traditions into your life to acknowledge and celebrate your blessings, fostering a routine of gratitude and remembrance?

_____
_____
_____
_____

Grace and gratitude are powerful tools for recognizing and celebrating the blessings in our lives. By focusing on abundance rather than scarcity, we cultivate a heart filled with contentment and joy. This shift in perspective not only enhances our personal well-being but also enriches our relationships and communities. As we acknowledge and celebrate our blessings, we create a positive cycle of gratitude that attracts even more abundance into our lives. Let us take time each day to reflect on the many gifts we receive, celebrate them with joy, and share them generously with others.

~Sanctifying the Meal~

Let's be honest—how many of us rush through our meals like we're competing in a speed-eating contest? We're busy, we're hungry, and we've got places to be. But what if we slowed down for just a moment? What if, before diving into that delicious plate of food, we took a deep breath and offered a simple prayer of thanks? Sanctifying a meal through prayer isn't just an old-fashioned tradition—it's a practice that transforms the ordinary act of eating into a moment of spiritual connection and gratitude. It's about recognizing that food is more than just fuel; it's a gift, and every meal is an opportunity to tap into something deeper.

Have you ever sat down to dinner after a long, hectic day? The food smells amazing, and your stomach is practically growling in anticipation. But instead of diving right in, you pause. You close your eyes, take a deep breath, and say a simple prayer of thanks. In that moment, something shifts. The chaos of the day fades away, and you're fully present, aware of the blessing that's right in front of you.

Sanctifying a meal isn't just about saying grace because it's what your grandma taught you to do. It's about hitting the pause button on life's hustle and bustle to acknowledge the true source of your sustenance. It's a moment to recognize that the food on your plate didn't just appear out of thin air—it's the result of countless hands and efforts, and ultimately, it's a gift from the divine.

When we take the time to sanctify our meals, we're making a powerful statement: This food, this moment, this act of nourishment—it matters. We're elevating the everyday to the sacred, reminding ourselves that even the simplest meal is worthy of reverence. And in doing so, we're cultivating a mindset of abundance and gratitude that can ripple out into every area of our lives.

You might be thinking, "Does saying a quick 'thank you' before eating really make that much of a difference?" The answer is a resounding yes! That small act of gratitude isn't just a polite gesture; it's a way of feeding your soul while you feed your body. When you sanctify your meal, you're opening up a channel of connection between you and the divine, inviting a sense of peace and presence into your daily routine.

Prayer before a meal is like seasoning for the soul—it adds flavor to the experience, making it richer and more fulfilling. It's a reminder that life is full of blessings, big and small, and that even in the midst of life's challenges, there's always something to be grateful for. By acknowledging the source of our sustenance, we're not just thanking God for the food itself, but for all the hands that helped bring it to our table—from the farmers and laborers to the cooks and servers.

This practice also deepens our connection with the divine. When we take a moment to sanctify our meals, we're essentially saying, "I see You in this. I recognize Your hand in my life, providing for me in ways both seen and unseen." It's a way of inviting the sacred into the mundane, transforming a simple meal into an act of worship and gratitude.

But the benefits of sanctifying your meal don't stop at the dinner table. This simple practice has a ripple effect, influencing your mindset and actions throughout the day. When you start your meal with gratitude, you're more likely to carry that sense of thankfulness into other areas of your life. You become more aware of the blessings that surround you, more attuned to the goodness that often goes unnoticed in the rush of daily life.

This practice can also help shift your focus from a mindset of scarcity—where you're constantly worried about what you don't have—to one of abundance, where you're grateful for what you do have. It's a subtle but powerful shift that can change the way you approach everything from your relationships to your work to your personal challenges.

And let's not forget the impact this can have on those around you. When you sanctify your meal, you're setting an example for others, showing them the value of pausing, reflecting, and giving thanks. It's a simple act, but it can inspire others to do the same, creating a culture of gratitude and reverence that extends beyond the table.

The Spiritual Significance of Sanctifying Meals

1. Acknowledging the Divine Source

How does recognizing God as the source of your sustenance affect your view of food and provision? In what moments can you pause to express gratitude for these gifts, understanding they come from the Creator? Reflect on how this awareness shapes your relationship with food and deepens your appreciation for life's blessings.

_____
_____
_____
_____
_____

Scriptural Reference:

- James 1:17 (NIV): *"Every good and perfect gift is from above, coming down from the Father of the heavenly lights, who does not change like shifting shadows."*

- This verse highlights the belief that all blessings, including our daily food, originate from a benevolent and unchanging divine source.

2. Setting the Meal Apart as Holy

How can you turn your meals into sacred acts by recognizing the interconnectedness of creation during mealtime prayers? In what ways does acknowledging the sacredness of your food deepen your respect for the earth's bounty and the labor involved? How might this practice enhance your appreciation for God's provision and foster greater gratitude and mindfulness in your daily life?

_____
_____
_____

3. Gratitude and Reflection
How can you incorporate gratitude and reflection into your mealtimes to deepen your appreciation for the nourishment you receive? Consider the journey of your food and express thanks for the meal and those who contributed to it. How might this mindfulness enhance your eating experience and strengthen your connection with God and your community? What steps can you take to cultivate a more thankful heart during meals?

4. Inviting the Divine Presence
How does inviting the divine into your mealtime prayers transform your perspective on everyday activities? Reflect on how acknowledging God's presence during meals deepens your spirituality and integrates faith into daily life. In what ways might this practice influence your actions and attitudes throughout the day?

Practical Ways to Sanctify Meals
1. Traditional Blessings and Prayers
How do traditional meal blessings, like saying grace in Christianity or Brachot in Judaism, enhance your sense of gratitude and sanctity while eating? How can incorporating

these practices into your mealtime routine strengthen your faith and deepen your appreciation for the nourishment you receive?

_____
_____
_____
_____

2. Personal Prayers and Reflections

How can you weave personal prayers and reflections into your daily routine to enrich your spiritual practice? Consider the blessings you're thankful for, recent impactful events, or individuals in need of prayer. In what ways can personalizing your prayers enhance their relevance and meaning, and how might this deepen your relationship with God while fostering empathy for others?

_____
_____
_____
_____

3. Creating a Sacred Space

How can you create a sacred space during mealtimes to enhance your spiritual experience? Consider elements like setting the table thoughtfully, using special dishes, or lighting candles to transform ordinary meals into meaningful moments. In what ways might these practices help you focus on the blessings of fellowship and deepen your reverence for the food and company you share?

_____
_____
_____
_____

Sanctifying a meal through prayer and reflection elevates the simple act of eating into a moment of spiritual connection and gratitude. By acknowledging the divine source of our sustenance and setting the meal apart as sacred, we deepen our appreciation for the blessings we receive and remember the interconnectedness of all creation. In a fast-paced world, taking the time to bless our food serves as a meaningful pause, a moment to slow down and fully immerse ourselves in the grace of the present.

When we bless a meal, we honor the many hands and hearts that contributed to bringing it to our plates—from the farmers and harvesters to those who prepared it with care. This gratitude cultivates humility, helping us recognize the web of life that supports us all. Sanctifying the meal, then, becomes an act of communal mindfulness, grounding us in a deeper awareness of our shared dependence on one another and on the earth.

This practice also encourages us to view all of life through a spiritual lens, reminding us that the divine is not limited to places of worship but is woven into our everyday experiences. Each time we bless a meal, we create a small altar of devotion in our hearts, nurturing a reverent spirit that permeates our entire day. This ongoing mindfulness inspires us to recognize the sacred not only in meals but in all our actions, conversations, and relationships.

As we consistently sanctify our meals, we deepen our connection with the Creator, inviting divine presence into the ordinary rhythms of our lives. It teaches us to live with a constant awareness of God's grace, making us more grateful, mindful, and attuned to the sacred rhythms of life. Over time, this practice transforms not only how we eat but how we live, helping us approach each moment with gratitude, wonder, and an ever-deepening connection to the divine source that sustains us all.

Sanctifying our meals also shifts our perspective on consumption, inviting us to consider the ethical and spiritual dimensions of our choices. When we pause to bless our food, we are reminded that our meals are not merely for personal satisfaction but also part of a larger, interconnected system. This recognition can inspire us to make more conscious choices about what and how we eat, seeking ways to honor creation by choosing foods that respect the earth, promote sustainability, and support those who labor within the food chain. Such intentional choices turn our meals into acts of stewardship, where every bite reflects our respect for God's creation and the people who contribute to it.

Furthermore, this practice deepens our sense of gratitude beyond the food itself, as it brings to mind God's continual provision and care for us. Food becomes a tangible reminder of God's goodness, and each meal becomes a moment to remember the abundance we often take for granted. This perspective encourages us to approach life with an open heart, sensitive to the many ways in which we are constantly blessed. The act of blessing our food can gradually cultivate a habit of gratitude that extends beyond the table, transforming our daily interactions, relationships, and activities into moments of thankfulness and awareness.

Finally, sanctifying our meals encourages us to cultivate a spirit of presence. In a world often consumed with speed and productivity, slowing down to honor our food becomes a practice of mindfulness, reminding us that life is not simply a series of tasks to complete but a sacred journey to experience. When we take the time to appreciate the food before us, we are practicing presence—choosing to savor each bite, each taste, each moment. This practice of slowing down nurtures our souls, helping us to live fully in each moment, attuned to the beauty and mystery that life holds. In this way, our meals become daily invitations to align ourselves with God's rhythms and to live with a heart full of reverence, wonder, and gratitude.

Chapter 4
Table Manners

Our first introduction to the world of manners is like a crash course in human civilization, where the wild, untamed child within us begins the journey of transformation into a refined member of society. And where does this grand initiation take place? More often than not, it begins at the table. This familiar setting, where meals are shared and conversations flow, becomes the arena where we graduate from being uncivilized brutes—those tiny tornadoes of crumbs and chaos—into well-mannered beings capable of surviving a formal dinner without embarrassing ourselves or our parents.

The rules we learn at the table are like the ABCs of human decency, the foundational lessons that shape our interactions with the world. "Wash your hands!"—that timeless commandment, reminding us that cleanliness isn't just a virtue but a prerequisite for being welcomed near anything edible. "Use your utensils properly!"—a gentle nudge towards civilization, teaching us that forks are meant for eating, not for jousting with our siblings. "Don't talk with your mouth full!"—a lesson in more than just hygiene; it's an early education in the art of communication, where we learn that speaking clearly and considerately matters, especially if we want our words to be heard without the added garnish of flying food particles. "Keep your elbows off the table!"—a seemingly arbitrary rule that hints at the broader principle of mindfulness, of being aware of how our actions affect those around us. And let's not forget, "Don't reach across the table!"—a crucial lesson in patience and courtesy, teaching us the importance of waiting our turn and respecting others' space.

The list of table manners might seem as long as the menu at a five-star restaurant, but each rule serves a greater purpose. The table isn't just a place to eat; it's the ultimate training ground for proper human conduct. It's where we first learn that we're not the center of the universe—that other people exist, and their needs and preferences matter too. At the table, we discover the significance of sharing, of taking turns, of considering others before diving for that last piece of bread (even when it's calling your name with an irresistible allure).

But the table is more than just a place to practice etiquette; it's a classroom where we learn valuable lessons about ourselves and others. It's where we begin to understand how to navigate social settings, how to engage in meaningful conversation, and how to truly listen to others. The table becomes a place where we experience the magic of connection, of breaking bread together and finding common ground, even when we disagree on who should get the biggest slice of cake.

At the table, we also learn to appreciate diversity—in tastes, preferences, and opinions. We come to realize that while some of us might be all about the mashed potatoes, others may live for the green beans, and that's perfectly okay. It's at the table that we practice respecting differences, learning to compromise, and making space for everyone, regardless of their preferences. The dining table becomes a microcosm of society, a place where we hone the skills that will carry us through life—patience, respect, empathy, and perhaps even a touch of diplomacy when there's only one piece of dessert left and everyone's eyeing it.

So, when we find ourselves gathered around a table, we should remember that it's more than just a place to eat. It's a place of transformation, where the uncivilized brute begins the journey to becoming a refined human being. It's where manners are not just about following rules but about learning how to live harmoniously with others. The table is where we learn that being civilized isn't merely about knowing which fork to use; it's about knowing how to treat the people around us with kindness, respect, and consideration.

In essence, the table is where we start to grasp the fundamentals of community living, where the seeds of civility are planted and nurtured. It's where we begin to understand that the real test of manners isn't in the flawless execution of etiquette but in the way we make others feel valued and respected. The lessons we learn at the table—lessons of gratitude, humility, and generosity—are the very lessons that prepare us to take our place in the broader world, ready to contribute to a society built on these enduring values.

~Gluttony is a Sin~

In an upper-middle-class suburb, shielded by manicured lawns and picket fences, one of the most horrifying cases of child neglect and abuse came to light. David and Louise Turpin, a seemingly ordinary couple, subjected their 13 children to unspeakable cruelty. They starved them, beat them, and deprived them of the most basic human needs: food, education, and love. This wasn't a case of poverty-driven desperation; they had more than enough resources to provide for their children. Yet, they chose to withhold, to torment, and to display their power by buying food, placing it on the table, and forcing their starving children to watch them eat. The perversity of this act lies in its cruelty and its unnecessary nature.

But when we look closely, we must ask ourselves: how different is this from the broader story of America? In a country where 20% of the population holds 86% of the wealth, while 1 in 5 children will go to bed hungry tonight, are we, as a society, any better than David and Louise Turpin?

We often distance ourselves from such extreme stories of abuse, seeing them as isolated incidents perpetrated by "monsters" who bear no resemblance to the rest of us. But perhaps what makes the Turpins' actions so chilling is not just their depravity, but how they mirror the structural cruelty embedded within our society. Just as the Turpins had the means to provide for their children but chose instead to flaunt their abundance in front of starving eyes, America is a nation with vast resources and wealth. Yet, we have systems that perpetuate inequality, hunger, and deprivation, even as others bask in excess.

The metaphor becomes disturbingly clear: a society that has the capacity to feed and care for every child but allows one in five children to go hungry is not much different from parents who starve their children while eating in front of them. We often view economic inequality in abstract terms—statistics and figures that make it easy to separate ourselves from the reality behind them. But when we strip away the numbers, we see a similar picture of power, control, and a cruel indifference to suffering.

The Turpins' behavior was not just neglect; it was the weaponization of abundance. They knew they had what their children needed and willfully withheld it to maintain control and instill fear. Similarly, the wealthiest sectors of our society often have more than enough—ample resources, food, and opportunities—yet they are withheld from the most vulnerable. Policies, economic systems, and cultural values have been structured in a way that allows a few to sit at a lavish table of plenty, while many others, including children, are left on the outside looking in, hungry for what should be their basic right.

We must confront the uncomfortable truth that systemic inequality and poverty are not natural disasters; they are human-made conditions. They are the result of decisions—often made by those in power—to prioritize profit, comfort, and status over the well-being of the collective. In that light, can we truly claim moral high ground over the Turpins when our society allows—and in some cases, designs—a reality where millions live in deprivation while a select few hoard more than they could ever need?

The question, then, isn't just about who is to blame but about the kind of society we want to build. Are we willing to continue living in a country where abundance and starvation coexist side by side, often within the same community? Are we content with a system that permits, and even normalizes, the economic equivalent of putting food on the table and forcing others to watch without offering a bite?

If we believe that the Turpins' actions were monstrous, then we must also be willing to examine the monstrosities within our own systems that allow child hunger, homelessness, and generational poverty to persist. True progress doesn't come from condemning individual acts of evil while ignoring the broader, systemic evils that impact millions. It comes from recognizing that we have the power and the resources to change these realities and choosing to do so.

To claim moral superiority over the Turpins is to absolve ourselves of responsibility for the structural inequities that harm so many in our own backyards. Perhaps the real question isn't, "Are we better than them?" but "What are we doing to be different?" If we are to build a society where every child has a seat at the table and enough to eat, then it starts with acknowledging the need for radical change—an overhaul of values that sees every human being as worthy of dignity, care, and love, not as an afterthought to profit and power.

We live in a world that loves to go big. Super-sized meals, all-you-can-eat buffets, and grocery carts overflowing with snacks—it's easy to see how gluttony can sneak its way into our lives without us even noticing. But before you reach for that third helping of dessert, let's take a moment to talk about why gluttony is more than just a bad habit—it's a sin. Yes, you heard that right. Gluttony, that old-fashioned word we usually associate with medieval feasts and overstuffed turkey dinners, is actually a serious issue. But don't worry; this isn't about guilt-tripping you out of enjoying your favorite foods. It's about understanding the bigger picture and how we can live healthier, more balanced, and more compassionate lives.

Gluttony is often misunderstood as simply eating too much, but it's deeper than that. At its core, gluttony is about excess—whether it's food, drink, or any other physical resource. It's that little voice that says, "More is better," even when you're already full. It's the impulse that drives you to consume, consume, consume, without stopping to consider the consequences. And the problem with gluttony isn't just what it does to your waistline—it's what it does to your soul.

When we give in to gluttony, we're essentially saying that our physical desires are more important than anything else. We're prioritizing short-term satisfaction over long-term well-being, and in doing so, we're neglecting our spiritual health. Gluttony reflects a lack of self-control, a disregard for the needs of others, and an overemphasis on satisfying our own appetites. It's the opposite of living a balanced, mindful, and generous life.

Now, let's flip the script. The covenant of provision, a divine promise of abundance and care, encourages us to approach life with a spirit of generosity rather than excess. Instead of hoarding resources or indulging in more than we need, the covenant calls us to share what we have, to think of others, and to use our blessings to make the world a better place.

Imagine a world where everyone lived by this principle. Instead of grabbing the last slice of pizza just because you can, you'd offer it to someone else—maybe someone who hasn't had enough. Instead of filling your plate to the brim at every meal, you'd take only what you need and leave the rest for others. By avoiding gluttony and embracing generosity, we're not just improving our own lives—we're contributing to a more equitable and compassionate community.

When we practice generosity, we're saying that we trust in the covenant of provision. We believe that there's enough to go around, that we don't have to hoard or overindulge because our needs will be met. Generosity is the antidote to gluttony, a way of turning our focus outward, away from our own desires and towards the needs of others. It's about finding balance, living within our means, and sharing our abundance with those who have less.

Let's break it down: Gluttony and generosity are two sides of the same coin, representing different ways of approaching life's abundance. Gluttony is all about "me, me, me"—it's a mindset of scarcity, where you're constantly worried that there won't be enough, so you grab as much as you can, whenever you can. It's the voice that tells you to eat that extra slice of cake, even though you're already stuffed, because what if there's no cake tomorrow?

Generosity, on the other hand, comes from a place of abundance. It's the mindset that says, "There's enough for everyone, including me." It's about trusting that your needs will be met, so you can afford to share with others. It's the voice that tells you to offer that extra slice of cake to someone else, knowing that doing so will bring joy to both of you.

When we choose generosity over gluttony, we're not just making better choices for our physical health—we're nurturing our spiritual health as well. We're cultivating self-control, practicing mindfulness, and building stronger connections with others. And let's be real: There's nothing more satisfying than knowing that you've made someone else's day a little brighter.

Here's the thing about generosity: It's contagious. When you choose to share, you inspire others to do the same. It creates a ripple effect that spreads through your community, leading to a more compassionate and caring world. Imagine if, instead of competing for the biggest portion or the best seat at the table, everyone focused on making sure that everyone else was taken care of. That's the kind of world the covenant of provision calls us to create—a world where generosity is the norm, not the exception.

And let's not forget the personal benefits of living generously. When you practice generosity, you're also practicing gratitude. You're recognizing that what you have is enough, and you're choosing to use your abundance to bless others. This mindset not only brings more joy into your life but also helps you develop a deeper sense of contentment and fulfillment.

Understanding Gluttony and Its Implications
1. The Nature of Gluttony
How does viewing gluttony as prioritizing personal desires over the needs of others prompt you to reflect on your habits? Recall a time when your desires overshadowed your responsibilities. What steps can you take to cultivate self-control and align your priorities with God's values? How might embracing this perspective lead to healthier relationships and a more fulfilling spiritual life?

_____
_____
_____
_____

Scriptural Reference:
- Proverbs 23:20-21 (NIV): *"Do not join those who drink too much wine or gorge themselves on meat, for drunkards and gluttons become poor, and drowsiness clothes them in rags."*
- This passage warns against excessive indulgence, highlighting the potential physical and social consequences of gluttony.

2. The Impact of Gluttony on Others

How does recognizing gluttony's impact on others challenge you to reevaluate your consumption habits? Consider how your choices in food, possessions, and resources affect those less fortunate. What practical steps can you take to shift from excess to generosity, promoting equity and justice in your community?

_____
_____
_____
_____
_____

The Virtue of Generosity

1. Generosity as a Response to Gluttony

How can you combat the temptation of gluttony by practicing generosity? Reflect on a recent moment when you prioritized your desires over others' needs. How can sharing your resources—such as time, talents, or material goods—promote the well-being of those around you? In what ways can your acts of generosity align with covenant values, fostering communal support and mutual care?

_____
_____
_____
_____
_____

Scriptural Reference:

- 2 Corinthians 9:6-7 (NIV): *"Remember this: Whoever sows sparingly will also reap sparingly, and whoever sows generously will also reap generously. Each of you should give what you have decided in your heart to give, not reluctantly or under compulsion, for God loves a cheerful giver."*
- This passage emphasizes the joy and rewards of giving generously, highlighting the positive outcomes of such behavior.

2. The Benefits of Generosity

How have you experienced the benefits of generosity as a giver or receiver? Reflect on a specific instance where your giving brought you joy. How can you cultivate a spirit of generosity in your daily life to bless others and enhance your emotional well-being? In what ways can this practice foster deeper connections and gratitude in your relationships?

_____
_____
_____
_____
_____

3. Generosity in Practice

Generosity can be practiced in many ways:

- **Sharing Resources:** Donating food, money, or goods to those in need.
- **Volunteering:** Offering time and skills to support charitable causes or community projects.
- **Acts of Kindness:** Small gestures, such as helping a neighbor or supporting a friend, also embody generosity.

_____
_____
_____
_____
_____

The Impact of Generosity on Communities

1. Building Stronger Communities

How can your acts of generosity help build stronger communities that foster care and support? Reflect on a time you witnessed community solidarity during a crisis. How can you intentionally share your resources and time to create a network of care that reflects Christ's love and strengthens community bonds?

_____
_____
_____
_____
_____

2. Reducing Inequity

How can you embody generosity to reduce social and economic inequities in your community? Reflect on your resources—time, talents, or finances—and consider how sharing them aligns with God's call for justice and care for the marginalized, fostering a more equitable society that reflects the heart of the covenant.

_____
_____
_____
_____
_____

3. Promoting a Culture of Gratitude

How can you promote a culture of gratitude in your relationships and community? Reflect on a recent act of generosity you received and its impact on you. How can you inspire others to express gratitude and continue the cycle of giving? Consider how your actions and words can cultivate appreciation, fostering deeper connections that reflect God's love.

_____
_____
_____

Gluttony, as a form of excessive indulgence and selfishness, disrupts the flow of provision and creates inequity. In contrast, the covenant teaches us to embrace generosity, sharing what we have to ensure that everyone has enough. Generosity not only fulfills a moral and spiritual obligation but also enriches our lives and strengthens our communities. By practicing generosity, we align ourselves with the values of the covenant, promoting justice, compassion, and communal well-being. Let us strive to live generously, recognizing that in giving, we not only bless others but also receive the joy and fulfillment that comes from being a cheerful giver.

> "The secret to living well and long is: eat half, walk double, laugh triple and love without measure" (Tibetan Proverb).

~Chew with Your Mouth Closed~

One of the worst culinary experiences is being at the dinner table, trying to enjoy a nice meal, when suddenly, you're hit with a sight that no one should have to endure—your dining companion's mouth wide open, mid-chew, looking like a scene from a wildlife documentary. Food is flying, and their shirt has unofficially become a full-body bib. It's a moment that makes you wish you could unsee things. And it's exactly why we've all been drilled with that timeless piece of advice: "Chew with your mouth closed!"

But here's the thing—this little rule, as much as it's about saving everyone from an unintentional show of your half-masticated meal, is about more than just good table manners. It's actually a pretty profound metaphor for how we should navigate life. Think about it: "Chew with your mouth closed" isn't just about keeping things neat and tidy at the dinner table; it's a lesson in respect, mindfulness, and common courtesy.

Let's start with respect. When you chew with your mouth closed, you're showing respect to the people around you. You're acknowledging that, hey, maybe they don't want to see or hear the inner workings of your lunch. In life, this translates to being aware of how our actions, however small, affect those around us. It's about being considerate, recognizing that we're all sharing this space—whether it's a dinner table or the wider world—and that a little thoughtfulness goes a long way.

Then there's mindfulness. Chewing with your mouth closed requires a bit of self-awareness. You've got to be in the moment, paying attention to what you're doing. It's a practice that, when applied to life, reminds us to slow down and be present. Whether we're eating, working, or interacting with others, being mindful helps us make better choices and fosters a deeper appreciation for the experiences we're having. Plus, when we're mindful, we're less likely to metaphorically (or literally) make a mess of things.

And let's not forget common courtesy. It's such a simple thing—closing your mouth while you chew—but it makes a big difference. It's one of those unwritten social contracts that, when followed, makes the world a little more pleasant for everyone. In life, common courtesy is the grease that keeps the gears of society running smoothly. It's holding the door open for someone, saying "please" and "thank you," and yes, chewing with your mouth closed. These small acts of consideration help create a more harmonious environment, where people feel respected and valued.

So, the next time you hear "Chew with your mouth closed!" think of it as more than just a rule to keep the peace at mealtime. It's a tiny phrase with big implications, reminding us that our actions, no matter how small, have an impact. Whether we're at the dinner table or navigating the complexities of life, the way we conduct ourselves matters. It's not just about avoiding grossing people out—it's about living with respect, mindfulness, and a good dose of common courtesy. And who knows? Maybe by embracing this simple rule, we'll make the world just a little bit better—one closed mouth at a time.

And lastly, chewing with our mouth closed is about something deeper— it's about resisting the urge to show off. Think about it: when we chew with our mouths closed, we're practicing a form of moderation. It's a subtle but powerful statement that we don't need to flaunt everything we've got—whether that's the contents of our lunch or the accomplishments of our lives. There's a quiet strength in modesty, a confidence that doesn't need to be bolstered by constant displays of what we possess. After all, no one really enjoys being around someone who's constantly showing off—it's like being forced to watch someone chew with their mouth open: uncomfortable and unnecessary.

Scripture has a lot to say about living modestly, and for good reason. Modesty isn't just about how we dress or how much we spend; it's a way of life that values humility over hubris, contentment over consumerism. When we live modestly, we're acknowledging that our worth isn't tied to what we have or how much we can show off. Instead, we're embracing a life that's focused on what truly matters—our character, our relationships, and our faith.

Chewing with our mouth closed is a small but significant way of embodying this principle. It's a reminder that we don't need to put everything on display. In a world that often encourages us to "go big or go home," to flaunt our success, our possessions, our every achievement, choosing to live modestly can be a radical act. It's about finding contentment in simplicity, about knowing that our value comes from who we are, not what we have or how much we can show.

When we live moderately, we're also freeing ourselves from the pressure to constantly keep up with others. It's easy to get caught up in the race to have the biggest, the best, the most impressive—whether it's our homes, our cars, or even our social media feeds. But when we choose modesty, we're stepping off that exhausting treadmill and embracing a life of peace and satisfaction. We're saying, "I have enough, and I am enough," and that's a powerful, liberating mindset.

Scriptures encourage us to live this way for a reason. Modesty isn't just about denying ourselves; it's about creating space for what truly matters. It's about focusing on the quality of our lives rather than the quantity of our possessions. It's about being grateful for what we have without feeling the need to constantly broadcast it to the world.

We should strive to remember that chewing with our mouth closed is more than just a good table manner—it's a small act of modesty. It's a way of living that values discretion over display, substance over style. And in that simple act, we can find a deeper lesson: that a life lived modestly, with humility and grace, is one that's truly rich—rich in what really counts.

The Importance of Respect

1. Respect for the Provision

How can practicing good manners at the table reflect your respect for the provisions and efforts behind your meals? Consider a recent meal and the people involved in bringing it to your table. How can you express gratitude for these blessings through your actions and attitude toward the provisions in your life? How might this awareness deepen your appreciation for God's generosity?

_____
_____
_____
_____
_____

Scriptural Reference:

- 1 Corinthians 10:31 (NIV): *"So whether you eat or drink or whatever you do, do it all for the glory of God."*

- This verse reminds us that all our actions, including how we conduct ourselves during meals, should honor and respect the divine provision.

2. Respect for Others

How can you show respect for others in daily interactions, especially during shared moments like mealtime? Reflect on a recent experience where your consideration—or lack thereof—affected those around you. What steps can you take to ensure your words and actions reflect genuine respect for others' feelings and boundaries, fostering a more harmonious environment?

_____
_____
_____
_____
_____

3. Building a Respectful Community

How can you contribute to building a respectful community in your circles, whether at home, work, or church? Reflect on a time when you felt valued by others. What specific actions can you take to show respect and appreciation, fostering an environment of trust and belonging that reflects Christ's love?

_____
_____
_____
_____
_____

The Role of Mindfulness

1. Mindfulness in Actions

How can you be more mindful in your daily actions and interactions, showing awareness and consideration for those around you? Reflect on a specific situation where you acted thoughtlessly. How can you practice mindfulness in small gestures, like dining etiquette, and larger decisions to honor God and positively influence others?

_____
_____
_____
_____
_____

2. Mindfulness in Communication

How can you practice mindful communication to deepen connections and understanding in your relationships? Reflect on a recent conversation with misunderstandings. What steps can you take to listen actively and respond thoughtfully, ensuring your words reflect Christ's compassion and respect for others?

_____
_____
_____
_____
_____

3. The Benefits of Mindfulness
How can cultivating mindfulness enhance your relationships and emotional well-being? Reflect on a recent overwhelming interaction. What mindfulness techniques can you use to approach future conversations with greater empathy and patience, embodying Christ's love and grace?

_____
_____
_____
_____
_____

Practical Applications
1. Observing Good Manners
How do your actions reflect your commitment to respect and mindfulness in your interactions? Recall a recent situation where good manners positively impacted a relationship. How can you intentionally incorporate acts of consideration into your daily life to honor God and those around you?

_____
_____
_____
_____

2. Practicing Active Listening

How can you practice active listening in your daily interactions to strengthen your relationships and show Christ's love? Reflect on a recent conversation where you could have listened better. What steps can you take to be more present and engaged in future discussions, fostering trust and respect?

_____
_____
_____
_____
_____

3. Being Present in Interactions

How can I be fully present in my interactions, such as during meals or conversations? What steps can I take to reduce distractions and deepen my engagement, enhancing my relationships and shared experiences?

_____
_____
_____
_____
_____

"Chew with your mouth closed" serves as a metaphor for the broader principles of respect and mindfulness that are integral to the covenant of provision. These principles encourage us to honor the blessings we receive, show consideration for others, and cultivate mindfulness in our daily actions. By practicing good manners, active listening, and being present, we contribute to a more respectful and mindful community. These practices not only enhance our own well-being but also create a positive and supportive environment for those around us. When we embrace these values, we foster a culture of care and attentiveness, where every individual feels seen, heard, and valued. In doing so, we uphold the covenant's call to live in harmony with one another, reflecting the divine intention of love and compassion in every interaction; refraining from the need to be exhibitionist and show offs,

The Table Book   Jermaine E. Pennington

stoking the flames of jealousy and stirring up a competitive spirit and comparison culture.

~Your Food Will Grow Cold Watching Someone Else's Plate~

Sitting at a table, eyes wandering over to someone else's plate, thinking, "Why didn't I order that?" or "Their meal looks so much better than mine!" But while we're busy drooling over someone else's dish, something unfortunate is happening: our own food is getting cold. And here's the thing—this little scenario is a metaphor for life. The saying *"Your food will grow cold watching someone else's plate"* is more than just a bit of wisdom for the dinner table; it's a powerful reminder to focus on and appreciate what we have rather than constantly comparing ourselves to others.

Here's the truth: someone else's plate might look better, but that doesn't mean it is better. Maybe their meal came with a side of vegetables you don't like, or maybe it's got a sauce that's way too spicy for your taste. In other words, what's perfect for someone else might not be perfect for you. The grass isn't always greener on the other side—it's just a different shade of green. And the sooner you realize that, the happier you'll be.

The same goes for life. It's easy to look at someone else's success, happiness, or even their material possessions and think they've got it all figured out. But everyone's journey is different, and what works for them might not work for you. Your blessings are tailored for you, just like your meal was cooked to your taste. Don't waste time wishing for what someone else has—focus on enjoying what's been served to you.

"Your food will grow cold watching someone else's plate" is more than just a cautionary phrase—it's a call to action. It's a reminder to stop comparing, start appreciating, and fully enjoy what's been served to you. Whether it's the meal in front of you or the life you're living, there's so much to savor if you just take the time to focus on it.

When the temptation to glance over at someone else's plate arises, remember this: what you have is enough. Your meal is delicious, your life is rich with blessings, and your journey is uniquely yours. Don't let your food grow cold or your joy fade because you're too busy looking at what someone else has. Instead, dig in, enjoy every bite, and celebrate the abundance that's right in front of you.

And who knows? Maybe the person sitting across from you is eyeing your plate, thinking they should've ordered what you've got. So, savor what's yours, because it was made just for you. Life is too short to spend it longing for someone else's meal—enjoy what's on your plate, because it's been perfectly seasoned just for you.

The Dangers of Comparisons

1. Envy and Dissatisfaction

How can I shift my focus from comparing myself to others to appreciating my unique blessings and achievements? What steps can I take to cultivate a mindset that celebrates my journey and fosters gratitude instead of feelings of inadequacy?

_____

_____

_____

_____

_____

Scriptural Reference:

- Proverbs 14:30 (NIV): *"A heart at peace gives life to the body, but envy rots the bones."*
- This verse highlights the destructive nature of envy and the peace that comes from contentment.

2. The Illusion of Perfection

How can I remind myself that social media often presents illusions of perfection that hide real struggles? In what ways can I cultivate authenticity and accept my own journey, understanding that true growth comes from embracing imperfection?

_____
_____
_____
_____
_____

3. The Loss of Focus

How has comparing myself to others distracted me from my own journey and goals? How can I refocus on my unique path and celebrate my progress to renew my motivation and purpose?

_____
_____
_____
_____
_____

The Importance of Contentment

1. Embracing Gratitude

How can embracing gratitude for what I have shift my perspective from scarcity to abundance? In what ways can I cultivate a spirit of gratitude to foster fulfillment and happiness?

_____
_____
_____
_____
_____

Scriptural Reference:

- Philippians 4:11-12 (NIV): *"I have learned to be content whatever the circumstances. I know what it is to be in need, and I know what it is to have plenty. I have learned the secret of being content in any and every situation."*

- This passage emphasizes the value of contentment and the ability to find peace and satisfaction regardless of external circumstances.

2. Finding Value in What We Have

How can I cultivate an appreciation for my own experiences, talents, and possessions, recognizing their unique value? In what ways can focusing on my personal growth and achievements help me find joy and contentment in my journey?

_____
_____
_____
_____
_____

3. The Freedom of Contentment

In what ways can I embrace contentment in my life, freeing myself from the pressures of comparison and competition? How might this shift towards authentic living enhance my sense of peace and self-acceptance?

_____
_____
_____
_____
_____

Practical Steps to Cultivate Contentment

1. Practice Gratitude Daily

How can I incorporate a daily practice of gratitude into my morning routine, and what specific blessings can I reflect on each day to cultivate a positive mindset? How might this practice transform my perspective throughout the day?

_____
_____
_____

2. Limit Exposure to Comparisons

How can I intentionally limit my exposure to comparisons, especially in media and social influences, and instead focus on positive and uplifting content that nurtures my well-being? What steps can I take to create a more supportive environment for my personal journey?

3. Reflect on Personal Growth

How can I take time to reflect on my personal growth and achievements, celebrating even the smallest milestones? In what ways can acknowledging my progress encourage me to continue moving forward on my journey?

4. Focus on Your Unique Path

In what ways can I honor and appreciate my unique journey, recognizing that it is distinct from others? How can I cultivate a spirit of contentment and purpose as I focus on my own goals and aspirations, rather than comparing myself to those around me?

"*Your food will grow cold watching someone else's plate*" serves as a metaphor for the dangers of comparisons and the importance of contentment. By focusing on what we have and cultivating gratitude, we can appreciate our own blessings and avoid the dissatisfaction that comes from constantly looking at others. Contentment brings peace, fulfillment, and freedom, allowing us to live authentically and joyfully. Let us embrace these principles in our daily lives, finding value in our unique journeys and celebrating the abundance we already possess.

~Don't Waste Food, Build a Longer Table~

Recently, as I was halfway through a bowl of spaghetti, a "Feed the Children" commercial flashed on the screen, claiming that 1 in 5 children in our country suffer from persistent hunger due to food insecurity. In the richest nation on earth, home to over 1,000 billionaires, we still struggle to feed our kids. The so-called "American Dream"—where wealth piles up in the hands of a few who couldn't spend it in 10,000 lifetimes—is harshly contrasted by an American Nightmare where hunger pains keep children awake at night.

Contemplate that you've just prepared a feast that could make a top chef envious. The table is bursting with dishes—some old favorites, some new experiments. But as the evening winds down, you notice the leftovers piling up, and before long, you're scraping perfectly good food into the trash. Sound familiar? We've all been there. But here's the thing—wasting food isn't just tossing out dinner; it's tossing aside the principles of stewardship and gratitude that lie at the heart of the covenant of provision. Instead of letting good food go to waste, why not build a longer table and share the abundance with others?

Let's face it—wasting food is a double-edged sword. You're not just throwing away something edible; you're discarding the time, effort, and resources that went into producing it. That bread you tossed? It started as a seed that someone planted, harvested, milled, baked, and delivered—all so it could end up in your trash can. When we waste food, we disregard the care and effort invested in every step of that process.

Wastefulness is a missed opportunity to honor the covenant of provision—a divine agreement calling us to be good stewards of the resources we've been given. When we waste food, we're saying, "I have more than enough, so I don't need to be mindful of what I have." But the abundance we enjoy isn't just for us; it's meant to be shared, to nourish not only our bodies but also the lives of others.

So, what's the solution? Simple: build a longer table, not a bigger trash can. When blessed with abundance, the best thing we can do is share it. Imagine if, instead of letting food go to waste, we invited more people to the table—family, friends, neighbors, even strangers. There's always room for one more chair, one more plate, one more person to share in the feast.

Building a longer table isn't just about feeding others—it's about creating community, fostering connection, and living out the principles of stewardship and gratitude. It's about realizing that our resources aren't ours to hoard but gifts to be shared. When we make room at the table for others, we're not just filling their stomachs; we're filling our lives with the joy that comes from generosity.

But sharing is only part of the solution—mindful consumption is another key ingredient in the recipe for a more grateful, generous life. When we're mindful of what we consume, we appreciate the food on our plates and are less likely to let it go to waste. It's about savoring each bite, taking only what we need, and being conscious of our consumption's impact on the world.

Mindful consumption also means planning ahead. Instead of cooking more than we can eat, why not prepare just enough? Instead of buying in bulk and letting half spoil, why not shop smart and buy only what we'll use? These small changes can make a big difference, not only in reducing waste but also in helping us develop a deeper appreciation for the food we have.

At the heart of it all is the covenant of provision, a divine promise that we'll always have what we need. But this promise comes with a responsibility: to be good stewards of what we're given, to use our resources wisely, and to share our abundance with others. When we avoid wastefulness and choose to build a longer table, we're living out this covenant in a meaningful way.

Gratitude isn't just about saying "thank you" for what we have—it's about showing our appreciation through our actions. It's about using our resources in a way that honors the Provider, being mindful of what we consume, and generous with what we share. When we live with this mindset, we're not only avoiding waste—we're creating a life filled with purpose, connection, and joy.

So, the next time you find yourself with more food than you know what to do with, remember this: Don't waste it—share it. Build a longer table, invite others to join in the feast, and savor every bite with gratitude. By being mindful of our consumption and generous with our abundance, we honor the covenant of provision and create a world where no one goes hungry and nothing goes to waste.

Food isn't just about filling our stomachs; it's about nourishing our souls, building community, and living out our values with every meal. So, let's make every bite count, every meal matter, and every table a place where everyone is welcome and well-fed.

The Problem of Food Waste

1. Understanding Food Waste

How can I deepen my understanding of the journey of food from production to my table, and in what ways can I actively reduce food waste in my life? What steps can I take to appreciate the resources involved in food production and honor them by being more mindful in my consumption habits?

_____

_____

_____

2. The Ethical Implications

How can I cultivate a deeper awareness of the ethical implications of food waste in my life? In what ways can I show appreciation for the labor and resources that go into food production, while also being more considerate of those who face hunger and food insecurity?

_____
_____
_____
_____

Scriptural Reference:

- Proverbs 12:27 (NIV): *"The lazy do not roast any game, but the diligent feed on the riches of the hunt."*
- This verse underscores the value of diligence and responsible use of resources, contrasting it with wastefulness.

The Importance of Stewardship

1. Stewardship and Responsibility

In what ways can I demonstrate good stewardship in my daily life, particularly in how I manage and care for the food and resources I have been given? How can planning my meals and using what I purchase reflect my responsibility to honor these gifts wisely?

_____
_____
_____
_____

2. The Spiritual Aspect of Stewardship

How does my understanding of stewardship reflect my relationship with the Creator and my gratitude for the gifts I have received? In what ways can I practice good stewardship to honor divine provision and acknowledge the blessings in my life?

3. Practical Steps for Reducing Waste

- Meal Planning: Plan meals to avoid buying excess food that may spoil.
- Proper Storage: Store food correctly to extend its shelf life and reduce spoilage.
- Creative Cooking: Use leftovers creatively to make new meals, minimizing waste.
- Mindful Portioning: Serve appropriate portions to avoid uneaten food.

The Value of Sharing

1. Sharing as an Act of Compassion

How can I view sharing food as a profound act of compassion and solidarity? In what specific ways can I ensure that my resources contribute to the well-being of others and strengthen the sense of community around me?

_____
_____
_____
_____
_____

2. The Joy of Generosity

How does embracing generosity, particularly in sharing food, enrich my life and the lives of others? In what ways can I actively practice generosity to foster joy, combat isolation, and strengthen my community?

_____
_____
_____

_____

_____

Scriptural Reference:

- Luke 3:11 (NIV): "John answered, *'Anyone who has two shirts should share with the one who has none, and anyone who has food should do the same.'*"
- This verse highlights the moral imperative to share our resources with those who are less fortunate.

3. Practical Ways to Share

- Donate to Food Banks: Donate non-perishable items or extra produce to local food banks.
- Community Meals: Participate in or organize community meals to share food and fellowship.
- Support Local Initiatives: Support local initiatives that provide meals to those in need, such as soup kitchens or community fridges.

The Role of Gratitude
1. Gratitude and Mindful Consumption
How can cultivating a spirit of gratitude for the food I have encourage me to consume wisely and respect the resources provided to me? In what ways does this appreciation foster contentment and help me resist the temptation to overconsume?

_____

_____

_____

_____

_____

2. Expressing Gratitude in Action
How can I express my gratitude through my actions, particularly in how I consume, reduce waste, and share with others? In what

ways does mindful living not only honor the blessings I have received but also positively impact my community and the environment?

_____

_____

_____

_____

"Don't Waste Food, Share" emphasizes the importance of mindful consumption and the value of sharing our resources. Wastefulness undermines the spirit of the covenant, while good stewardship and generosity honor the provision we receive. By practicing stewardship and sharing what we have, we demonstrate gratitude and compassion, contributing to a more equitable and caring community. Let us strive to be mindful of our consumption habits, reduce waste, and share generously, reflecting the values of the covenant in our daily lives.

~Don't Break Your Plate~

Imagine sitting down to a beautiful meal, the table set with care, everything in its place. You're about to dig in when—whoops!—you drop your plate, and it shatters into a million pieces. Not exactly the start you were hoping for, right? But here's the thing: "Don't Break Your Plate" is more than just a warning to avoid kitchen disasters. It's a metaphor for something much deeper—a reminder to take care of the possessions and resources we've been given, and to treat them with the respect and mindfulness they deserve.

In the literal sense, breaking your plate is, well, a bit of a mess. It's a small disaster that turns a perfectly good meal into a scramble to clean up shards of ceramic. But metaphorically, "Don't Break Your Plate" is about much more than avoiding accidents. It's about recognizing the value of what we have and being mindful of how we use and care for our resources.

Your plate, in this sense, represents all the provisions and blessings you've received in life—whether it's your food, your possessions, or even your relationships. Just like that plate, these things are fragile, valuable, and deserving of care. When you break your plate, metaphorically speaking, you're failing to appreciate and protect what's been given to you. You're taking for granted the resources at your disposal, rather than treating them with the respect and gratitude they deserve.

"Don't Break Your Plate" is a call to action—a reminder to live with mindfulness and respect in every aspect of our lives. It's about more than just being careful with our dishes; it's about being careful with everything we've been entrusted with. Whether it's your time, your money, your health, or your relationships, the principle is the same: take care of what you have, and don't let it slip through your fingers.

This principle extends to the way we consume and enjoy our meals. Eating isn't just about satisfying hunger; it's an opportunity to practice gratitude and mindfulness. When you sit down to eat, you're not just fueling your body—you're participating in a ritual that connects you to the earth, to the people who prepared your food, and to the traditions that have shaped your life. By taking care of your plate—literally and figuratively—you're honoring the effort and resources that went into your meal, and you're recognizing the importance of these moments in your daily life.

Gratitude isn't just a feeling; it's an action. It's something you demonstrate through the way you treat the things and people in your life. When you care for what you have, you're showing that you value it, that you're thankful for it, and that you understand its importance. This is true whether you're taking care of your possessions, your food, or your relationships.

Imagine you've been given a beautiful, handmade plate—something unique and irreplaceable. You wouldn't toss it around carelessly or leave it in the sink to chip and crack. You'd handle it with care, appreciating its craftsmanship and the thought that went into it. In the same way, we should treat all of our resources and blessings with care, recognizing that they are gifts that deserve our respect.

This extends to how we manage the food on our plates. Don't take more than you can eat; don't let food go to waste. By being mindful of our consumption, we honor the food itself, the people who prepared it, and the earth that provided it. It's about being present in the moment, appreciating the meal before you, and recognizing that every bite is a blessing.

Living by the "Don't Break Your Plate" principle means adopting a mindset of mindfulness and appreciation in all areas of life. It's about being conscious of the way you interact with the world, the way you treat your possessions, and the way you care for your resources. When you take the time to cherish what you have, you're not only protecting it—you're enriching your own life.

Consider this: when you're mindful of your actions, when you care for your belongings, and when you treat every meal as a moment to be grateful, you're cultivating a life filled with purpose and satisfaction. You're avoiding the pitfalls of wastefulness, carelessness, and ingratitude, and instead, you're building a life that's grounded in respect, mindfulness, and joy.

So, the next time you sit down to a meal—or find yourself taking care of something valuable—remember the phrase, "Don't Break Your Plate." It's a simple reminder that the way we treat our resources reflects our appreciation for the blessings we've received. By living with care and gratitude, we honor the provisions in our lives and create a richer, more fulfilling existence.

After all, life is full of fragile, precious moments—just like that plate in your hands. So take care of it, cherish it, and let it remind you to approach each day with mindfulness, respect, and a heart full of gratitude.

The Importance of Caring for Our Possessions
1. Respect for the Provision

How can my care for everyday possessions, like plates, reflect a deeper respect for the resources and efforts that went into their creation? In what ways can this appreciation help me minimize waste and honor the provisions I have received?

_____
_____
_____
_____
_____

2. Gratitude and Mindfulness

How can cultivating gratitude and mindfulness in my care for possessions enhance my appreciation for their role in my life? In what ways might this practice deepen my sense of contentment and responsibility toward what I own?

_____
_____
_____
_____
_____

Scriptural Reference:

- Luke 16:10 (NIV): *"Whoever can be trusted with very little can also be trusted with much, and whoever is dishonest with very little will also be dishonest with much."*

- This verse emphasizes the importance of being responsible with even the smallest of resources, highlighting the broader implications of stewardship.

3. The Practical Benefits of Maintenance

How does regular maintenance of my possessions reflect my commitment to stewardship and sustainable living? In what ways can I incorporate mindful care into my daily routine to extend the life of the things I own while minimizing my environmental impact?

Symbolic Meaning of "Don't Break Your Plate"

1. The Act of Eating as a Sacred Ritual

How can I elevate the act of eating to a sacred ritual in my life? In what ways can taking care of the tools and spaces we use for meals deepen my appreciation for the nourishment I receive and the community shared during these moments?

2. Responsibility and Stewardship

How can I practice responsibility and stewardship in my daily life, ensuring that I care for my resources—time, energy, and relationships—mindfully and thoughtfully? In what ways can this commitment to stewardship enhance my relationships and contribute to a greater sense of community?

3. Avoiding Waste and Overconsumption

In what ways can I cultivate a mindset that values my possessions, helping me to avoid waste and overconsumption? How might this shift in perspective contribute to sustainability and a deeper appreciation for what I have?

_____
_____
_____
_____
_____

Practical Applications

1. Regular Maintenance and Care

How can I practice regular maintenance and care for the items in my home? In what specific ways can I handle my possessions with intention to ensure their longevity and show gratitude for what I have?

_____
_____
_____
_____

2. Mindful Consumption

How can I cultivate a mindset of mindful consumption in my life? In what ways can I evaluate my purchases to ensure they are necessary and align with my values, prioritizing quality and durability over quantity?

_____
_____
_____
_____

3. Promoting a Culture of Care

How can I actively promote a culture of care and responsibility within my community or household? In what ways can I educate others about the importance of taking care of our shared spaces and resources while leading by example through my own actions?

_____
_____
_____
_____
_____

4. Environmental Considerations

How can I become more mindful of my consumption choices and their environmental impact? In what ways can I choose sustainably produced or eco-friendly products to contribute to the well-being of the planet?

_____
_____
_____
_____

"Don't Break Your Plate" is a reminder to take care of the resources and possessions we are blessed with. This principle underscores the importance of respect, gratitude, and mindfulness in our daily lives. By caring for our belongings, we not only honor the provision we receive but also promote sustainability and responsible living. This practice extends to all aspects of our lives, encouraging us to be good stewards of our time, energy, and relationships. Let us embrace the values of care and maintenance, reflecting our respect for the resources entrusted to us and our commitment to a mindful and sustainable lifestyle.

~Set the Table Right, and the Meal Will Follow: A Path Forward in Conflict Resolution~

There's wisdom in the old adage, *"Set the table right, and the meal will follow."* It implies that preparation and planning are essential to success—whether you're preparing a meal, setting goals, or navigating the complexities of relationships. I want to extend this idea into the realm of peacemaking, both in our personal lives and in the broader world. The work of peacemaking becomes an exercise in futility if we cannot first secure our own inner peace. Inner peace is about quieting the noise within us, calming the internal chaos, and finding a grounded state of being. Peace isn't something that just happens by accident; it must be intentionally pursued and cultivated. As Brian Hardin insightfully remarks, *"When it comes to experiencing peace, we can't cram it in at the last minute; we need to build a foundation for it by making God central in our lives."*

Starting with Inner Peace: The Foundation for Resolving Conflict

The journey to resolving conflict begins with ourselves. How can we hope to bring peace to any situation if we are internally unsettled, reactive, or on edge? Inner peace requires us to silence the internal noise—the anxieties, fears, and ego-driven thoughts that disrupt our equilibrium. It's about finding calm amid chaos, allowing us to approach conflicts with clarity, compassion, and understanding rather than from a place of frustration or defensiveness.

To cultivate inner peace, we must build a solid foundation. This starts with centering ourselves—whether through prayer, meditation, or simply taking time to reflect and breathe. Making God or a higher purpose central in our lives gives us a steady anchor, a sense of groundedness that doesn't easily sway with the winds of conflict. This foundation allows us to enter into conversations and confrontations with a spirit of peace rather than turmoil.

The "Peace Table" Approach: Creating a Sacred Space for Resolution

When my wife and I were newly married, we hit a rough patch that led us to seek counseling. One invaluable piece of advice from our therapist was to designate a specific place in our home—a "peace table"—where we could address conflicts. The idea was simple but profound: rather than allowing disputes to erupt spontaneously in any room and contaminate the entire home with tension, we would make appointments to tackle difficult conversations at the peace table. This small but intentional step made a significant difference.

> 1. **Creating a Designated Space for Dialogue:** Setting up a "peace table" in our homes, offices, or communities is more than a physical arrangement; it symbolizes a commitment to

healthy dialogue. This dedicated space becomes a neutral ground, free from distractions and charged emotions, where conflicts can be discussed thoughtfully and intentionally. It's like setting the table for a meal—you prepare the space, choose the right ingredients (words), and ensure that the setting is conducive to sharing (listening).

2. Setting Clear Boundaries: Just as a table has defined edges, so too must our conflict resolution efforts. Setting boundaries helps create a sense of safety and respect, making it easier for everyone involved to express themselves without fear of attack or escalation. It also involves agreeing on ground rules: no interrupting, no raised voices, and no personal attacks. The peace table becomes a place where both parties know the rules of engagement and are committed to honoring them.

3. Scheduling the Conversation: Rather than allowing conflicts to catch us off guard or fester into bigger issues, we can schedule time to address them. This allows both parties to prepare mentally and emotionally, reducing the likelihood of reactive, heated responses. Just as we would prepare for a meaningful meal, we prepare ourselves to come to the table with an open mind and a willingness to understand, not just to be understood.

Building Bridges, Not Walls: The Power of Togetherness in Conflict Resolution

When we set the table right for conflict resolution, we create opportunities to build bridges instead of walls. Coming together with the intention of listening, understanding, and finding common ground transforms what could be a divisive encounter into a unifying experience.

1. The Power of Listening: At the peace table, listening becomes an act of love and humility. Instead of planning our next rebuttal, we listen to understand the other person's perspective. This doesn't mean we have to agree with everything they say, but it shows that we value their voice and experience. Listening with empathy can diffuse tension and open the door to genuine reconciliation.

2. Focusing on Shared Goals: Just as a meal is more enjoyable when everyone is hungry for connection, conflict resolution is more effective when both parties are committed to a shared goal—be it peace, harmony, or mutual understanding. At the peace table, we focus not on winning the argument but on finding a way forward together. We ask ourselves, "What do we both want to achieve here?" and work towards that common objective.

3. Embracing Vulnerability and Honesty: The peace table is a space where we lay down our defenses and speak from the heart. This requires vulnerability and honesty—acknowledging our own shortcomings, fears, and hopes. It's about saying, "I want us to move forward, and I'm willing to be open about where I've gone wrong." This kind of transparency fosters trust and paves the way for genuine resolution.

A Path Forward: Creating More "Peace Tables" in Our Lives

The concept of the peace table is one that can be expanded far beyond the walls of our homes. Imagine applying this idea in our workplaces, communities, and even larger societal contexts. Instead of letting conflicts simmer or explode into hostility, we create spaces—physical or metaphorical—where dialogue and understanding are prioritized over division and discord.

1. Peace Tables in the Workplace: Create meeting spaces specifically for conflict resolution, where team members can come together to discuss differences openly and respectfully. This could be a quiet room with comfortable seating, where the environment itself encourages calm and constructive dialogue.

2. Community Peace Tables: In communities, peace tables could be established in local centers, churches, or parks—places where neighbors, community leaders, and members can come together to address issues that impact their collective well-being.

3. Global Peace Tables: On a larger scale, the idea of the peace table can inspire diplomatic approaches to resolving international conflicts. Imagine a world where leaders regularly meet not to negotiate power but to genuinely understand each other's perspectives, prioritize peace, and seek common ground.

The Meal of Peace Will Follow
Setting the table right doesn't guarantee that every conflict will be resolved perfectly or immediately. But it does ensure that the conditions are right for peace to have a seat at the table. When we commit to building peace from the inside out—starting with our inner peace and extending it to every interaction—we create the foundation for a world where conflict is not something to be feared but a process that leads us to greater understanding and connection.

So, let's set our tables right—both literally and figuratively. Let's be intentional about creating spaces for peace, where every person feels heard, valued, and ready to share in the meal of reconciliation. When we do this, we build a path forward that is rich with possibility, where the meal that follows is one of unity, understanding, and lasting peace.

Chapter 5
Guess Who's Coming to Dinner

"Guess Who's Coming to Dinner" isn't just the title of a classic 1967 film; it's a cultural lightning rod that electrified the American conscience. Starring the legendary Sidney Poitier and Katharine Hepburn, this romantic comedy-drama did more than entertain—it boldly challenged the social norms of its time. In an era when interracial marriage was still a flashpoint of controversy, this film was nothing short of revolutionary. It portrayed an interracial couple not just with acceptance, but with dignity and warmth, at a time when such unions were still illegal in 17 states. This was no small feat; it was a cinematic declaration of love in defiance of the law, filmed just before the Supreme Court's landmark decision in Loving v. Virginia struck down anti-miscegenation laws forever.

The release of *"Guess Who's Coming to Dinner"* was a societal earthquake that shook the consciousness of our nation to its racist core. It didn't just invite the audience to the table—it flipped the table over. The title itself has since become a symbol, a phrase that suggests more than just an unexpected guest—it hints at the seismic shift that occurs when deeply entrenched barriers of race, culture, and prejudice are torn down.

To invoke *"Guess Who's Coming to Dinner"* today is to suggest a moment of reckoning, a bold, perhaps uncomfortable, but ultimately necessary confrontation with the status quo. It's about those moments that force society to gasp in collective shock and, hopefully, breathe out in relief as the walls of segregation and division crumble. The phrase embodies the idea of welcoming the unexpected, embracing change, and challenging the conventions that have kept us divided for far too long.

In today's world, where conversations about race, equality, and justice continue to evolve, *"Guess Who's Coming to Dinner"* remains a powerful metaphor. It's a reminder that true progress often begins with a moment of discomfort—a moment where we are forced to see the world from a different perspective, to share a meal with those we might never have imagined breaking bread with, and to realize that the dinner table, like society itself, is big enough for everyone.

Two thousand years ago, Jesus had a habit of turning the social order on its head—starting with where He chose to sit down for a meal. Jesus, a respected Rabbi, expected to uphold the highest standards of purity and propriety, deliberately pulls up a chair at tables that made society cringe. He dined with prostitutes, tax collectors, and other so-called "undesirables." It was scandalous. The religious elite were left clutching their pearls, horrified that this man of God would tarnish His reputation by breaking bread with those who were deemed beyond redemption.

But Jesus wasn't just being rebellious for the sake of it. He was making a profound statement—one that shook the very foundations of the establishment. As He shared meals with those on the margins, He began to speak of the Kingdom of God in a way that was as radical as it was unsettling. He didn't just tolerate these outcasts; He declared that the Kingdom was made with them in mind. Imagine the shockwaves this sent through the Pharisees, Sadducees, Zealots, and other religious gatekeepers. They couldn't fathom a kingdom where the last, the lost, and the least had reserved seats at the table—let alone the best seats in the house.

Jesus wasn't just dining with sinners; He was casting a vision for a new kind of community—one that flipped the script on who belongs and who doesn't. He exposed the hypocrisy of a society that claimed to love God but shunned those God loves. By sitting with the outcasts, He demonstrated that the Kingdom of God is not a gated community for the religiously elite, but an open table where everyone is welcome, especially those whom the world has rejected.

In doing so, Jesus embarrassed the establishment not with uncouth behavior, but with a radical grace that they couldn't understand. He showed that God's table is not reserved for the righteous alone, but set for all who hunger for something more—no matter their past, no matter their status. And in this, He wasn't just offering a meal; He was offering a place in a kingdom where the first will be last, and the last will be first—a kingdom where everyone, even those society frowns upon, has a place of honor.

Mia Carella beautifully captures the essence of true inclusion when she says, *"Inclusion isn't just inviting someone to sit at your table. It's believing they belong there."* This statement challenges us to go beyond mere gestures of kindness or token invitations. Real inclusion is about recognizing the inherent value and worth of each individual and affirming that they have a rightful place at the table—no questions asked. It's about more than making room; it's about making people feel that they are fully welcome, wanted, and worthy of being there.

No one exemplified this kind of radical inclusion better than Jesus. By embracing the Jesus model, we are called to do more than just open our doors; we are invited to open our hearts. It means standing up against exclusion, challenging our own biases, and intentionally creating spaces where everyone feels they belong. When we believe that every person at our table has something unique and beautiful to offer, we create a culture where diversity is celebrated and everyone thrives. Inclusion, then, becomes more than an act of kindness; it becomes a way of life that can transform our communities, our workplaces, and our world. It reminds us that, like Jesus, we too have the power to affirm humanity by saying to everyone we meet, "You belong here."

~The Last~

The covenant of provision is a profound expression of God's inclusive and compassionate love, extending its promises to every person, especially those who are marginalized and overlooked in society. This covenant is not limited to those who are privileged or powerful; rather, it reaches out to "the last"—those who are often forgotten, undervalued, or excluded due to their socio-economic status, cultural background, or personal circumstances.

In the framework of this covenant, "the last" are not merely acknowledged as an afterthought. They are actively welcomed and honored at the table, where their inherent dignity and worth are affirmed. This is not just a gesture of inclusion but a radical reordering of values, where the least esteemed by the world are given a place of prominence in the eyes of God.

The concept of "the last" in this context refers to individuals and groups who, for various reasons, find themselves on the margins of society. These are the people who often face systemic injustices, who struggle against the weight of poverty, discrimination, or neglect. They may be the poor, the oppressed, the refugees, the disabled, the elderly, or those from minority communities. Their voices are often silenced, their needs ignored, and their contributions undervalued.

However, the covenant of provision calls for a profound recognition of their worth. It reminds us that every person is made in the image of God, and therefore, every person is deserving of dignity and respect. This covenant is a declaration that no one is beyond the reach of God's love and care, and that society's tendency to overlook or marginalize certain individuals is in direct conflict with the values of the Kingdom of God.

In the spirit of the covenant of provision, those who are last in the eyes of the world are given a place of honor at the table. This is more than just a symbolic gesture; it is a powerful statement about the way God's Kingdom operates. In a world that often values wealth, status, and power, the covenant of provision turns these values upside down. It proclaims that those who are last shall be first, and that the true measure of a society is how it treats its most vulnerable members.

To welcome and honor "the last" at the table is to acknowledge their humanity in its fullness. It is to see beyond the labels and stereotypes that society imposes and to recognize the unique gifts and perspectives that each person brings. It is to affirm that every person, regardless of their circumstances, has something valuable to contribute to the community. This act of inclusion is not about charity; it is about justice. It is about creating a space where everyone is valued and where everyone's needs are met.

The covenant of provision challenges us to build a society that reflects these values of inclusion and compassion. It calls us to examine the ways in which we may unconsciously perpetuate systems of exclusion and to take concrete steps to ensure that no one is left behind. This involves not only addressing the immediate needs of those who are marginalized but also working to dismantle the structural inequalities that keep them on the margins.

In practice, this means advocating for policies that protect the rights and dignity of the most vulnerable, supporting initiatives that provide access to education, healthcare, and economic opportunities, and creating communities where diversity is celebrated and everyone is welcomed. It also means cultivating a personal and collective commitment to seeing and serving "the last," not as a burden but as a sacred duty and privilege.

At the heart of the covenant of provision is the affirmation of each person's dignity and worth. This covenant reminds us that every individual, regardless of their position in society, is deeply loved by God and is an integral part of the human family. It calls us to look beyond our own comfort and privilege and to extend our hands and hearts to those who are often excluded.

In honoring "the last," we are living out the true essence of the covenant. We are participating in the work of God's Kingdom, where the first shall be last, and the last shall be first. This is a Kingdom where love, justice, and compassion reign, and where every person has a place at the table.

The covenant of provision offers us a vision of a more inclusive and compassionate world, where the marginalized are not only included but are honored and uplifted. It challenges us to live in a way that reflects the values of God's Kingdom, where every person's dignity is recognized, and where love and justice guide our actions.

As we embrace this covenant, we are called to be agents of change in our communities, working to create a society where all are welcomed, all are valued, and all are provided for. In doing so, we honor the spirit of the covenant and help bring about the world that God envisions—a world where everyone, especially "the last," has a place at the table.

The Significance of "The Last"

1. Recognizing the Marginalized

How can I better recognize and acknowledge the experiences of marginalized individuals in my community? What actions can I take to address the systemic barriers they face and advocate for their access to resources, opportunities, and basic rights?

_____
_____
_____
_____
_____

2. The Call to Inclusion

How can I respond to the call for inclusion in my community by ensuring that everyone, regardless of their status or circumstances, has a place at the table? What steps can I take to embody the values of compassion, justice, and equality in my interactions with others?

_____
_____
_____
_____
_____

Scriptural Reference:

- Matthew 20:16 (NIV): *"So the last will be first, and the first will be last."*
- This verse highlights the reversal of societal norms in the kingdom of God, where those who are marginalized are given priority and honor.

3. Honoring the Dignity of All

How can I actively honor the dignity and worth of every individual in my community, especially those who are often overlooked? In what ways can treating others with respect and valuing their contributions help create a more just and compassionate environment?

___
___
___
___
___

The Transformative Impact of Inclusion

1. Empowerment and Recognition

In what ways can I help empower and recognize the strengths of marginalized individuals in my community, ensuring their voices are heard and their contributions valued? How might this recognition impact both their self-esteem and our collective growth?

___
___
___
___
___

2. Building Stronger Communities

How can I actively contribute to creating a more inclusive community that honors the marginalized, and in what ways might this effort strengthen our collective resilience and enrich our shared experiences?

___
___
___
___
___

3. Reflecting Divine Compassion

In what ways can I extend divine compassion to marginalized individuals in my community, and how might this practice deepen my own spiritual journey and strengthen the moral fabric of our collective faith?

_____
_____
_____
_____
_____

Scriptural Reference:

- Luke 14:13-14 (NIV): *"But when you give a banquet, invite the poor, the crippled, the lame, the blind, and you will be blessed. Although they cannot repay you, you will be repaid at the resurrection of the righteous."*
- This passage underscores the importance of including and serving those who are often excluded or overlooked.

Practical Steps for Inclusion

1. Creating Welcoming Spaces

How can I contribute to creating welcoming spaces that ensure everyone, especially marginalized individuals, feels safe, valued, and included?

_____
_____
_____
_____
_____

2. Listening and Responding

In what ways can I practice active listening and engage in empathetic dialogue to better understand and respond to the needs of marginalized individuals and communities?

_____
_____
_____

3. Advocacy and Support

How can I actively advocate for policies and support initiatives that promote equity and justice for marginalized groups in my community?

4. Celebrating Diversity

In what ways can I actively celebrate and honor the diversity within my community, ensuring that different cultures, traditions, and experiences are recognized and appreciated?

"The Last" emphasizes the inclusive nature of the covenant of provision, which extends to the marginalized and overlooked. By welcoming and honoring the last at the table, we affirm their dignity and worth, challenge societal inequalities, and reflect the values of compassion and justice. Inclusion not only benefits those who are marginalized but also enriches the entire community, fostering a culture of respect, empathy, and solidarity. Let us commit to creating a world where everyone, especially the last, is welcomed, valued, and honored, embodying the true spirit of the covenant. And the "Last" can be assured that even if they arrive late to dinner, at God's table of provision, there will always be more than enough to satisfy their appetite, for there is no scarcity in the Kingdom of God.

~The Lost~

The covenant of provision is more than just a promise of material sustenance; it is a profound, compassionate call that extends far beyond the tangible. At its core, this covenant offers a warm invitation to "the lost"—those who have strayed from their paths, who feel disconnected from their communities, or who find themselves isolated from purpose and belonging. This invitation is not merely an offer to fill an empty plate; it is a powerful gesture of love and inclusion, a call to bring everyone back to the table—a place of reunion, healing, and restoration.

In the context of this covenant, "the lost" refers to those who are spiritually disconnected from God and living without the guidance, purpose, and relationship that come from knowing Him as well as those who feels separated from the fabric of community. They may be individuals who have wandered away from their spiritual roots, those who have been alienated by circumstances beyond their control, or those who have gradually become disconnected from a sense of meaning in their lives. The lost are not just those who are geographically distant, but also those who feel emotionally, spiritually, or socially adrift.

This disconnection can arise from various sources: personal failures, societal rejection, mental or emotional struggles, or the overwhelming pressures of life. Regardless of the cause, the experience of being lost is marked by a deep sense of isolation, a feeling of being adrift without a clear path back to wholeness. It is a state of yearning for connection, for a place where one is seen, valued, and understood.

The covenant of provision is inherently inclusive, rooted in a deep compassion that mirrors the restorative nature of divine love. It does not simply wait for the lost to find their way back; it actively reaches out, extending a hand to guide them home. This covenant recognizes that no one is beyond the reach of restoration, and it emphasizes that every individual, no matter how far they have strayed, is worthy of love, dignity, and a place at the table.

This invitation to the lost is not just an act of charity; it is a recognition of the fundamental truth that every person is valuable and that their presence is essential to the completeness of the community. The covenant's call is a reminder that the table is not whole until all who are lost have been found and welcomed back. It is an affirmation that everyone, regardless of their past or present circumstances, has a place where they belong.

Inclusion is more than just allowing someone to occupy a space; it is about actively welcoming them, embracing their unique journey, and offering a genuine sense of belonging. For the lost, this inclusion is not just healing—it is transformative. It turns isolation into connection, despair into hope, and confusion into clarity.

When the lost are welcomed back to the table, they are not only fed but also nourished in a deeper, more profound way. They are given the opportunity to reconnect with their true selves, to rediscover their purpose, and to rebuild the relationships that give their lives meaning. The act of inclusion becomes a powerful force for healing, as it helps to mend the fractures that have caused their sense of lostness.

Moreover, this inclusion is not conditional; it does not require the lost to first "fix" themselves or prove their worth. Instead, it meets them exactly where they are, offering acceptance and love as the foundation for their restoration. This is the essence of the covenant's compassion—an unconditional love that seeks to heal and restore, rather than to judge or exclude.

Reunion and restoration are at the heart of the covenant of provision. The act of bringing the lost back to the table is not just about filling an empty seat; it is about restoring wholeness to the individual and to the community. It is about repairing the bonds that have been broken and creating a space where every person is valued and every voice is heard.

For the lost, this reunion can be a life-changing experience. It offers a chance to start anew, to reclaim their identity and purpose, and to find a sense of belonging that may have been missing for years. The act of being welcomed back, of being invited to share in the feast, is a powerful affirmation of their worth and a testament to the enduring love that the covenant represents.

But the impact of this reunion extends beyond the individual. When the lost are restored, the entire community is enriched. Their return brings new perspectives, experiences, and strengths that enhance the collective well-being of the group. The act of restoration strengthens the bonds of the community, creating a deeper sense of unity and shared purpose.

The covenant of provision is a profound expression of inclusive love and compassion, one that reaches out to the lost with a promise of reunion and restoration. It is a call to recognize the inherent dignity of every person, to offer a place of belonging to those who feel disconnected, and to heal the wounds of isolation with the balm of inclusion.

As we embrace this covenant, we are invited to actively participate in the work of restoration—to extend our tables, to open our hearts, and to welcome the lost back into the fold. In doing so, we honor the true spirit of the covenant, creating a community where everyone is seen, valued, and loved—a place where no one is ever truly lost, but where all are found and brought home. This act of restoration calls us to be agents of grace, reaching out to those on the margins, and offering a seat at the table of belonging. It challenges us to break down barriers of division and exclusion, fostering a spirit of unity that reflects the boundless love of the Creator. In this way, we become co-laborers in God's redemptive work, building a world that mirrors the inclusive and transformative nature of His covenant, where every person is embraced as part of the family and every story is woven into the larger tapestry of God's love and purpose.

The Significance of "The Lost"
1. Understanding Disconnection
What steps can I take to better understand and reach out to those who feel disconnected from their communities or spiritual beliefs, recognizing their struggles and helping them find purpose and belonging?

2. The Call to Return

How can I embody the values of forgiveness, grace, and unconditional love in my life, creating an environment that welcomes those who have strayed back to the table?

Scriptural Reference:

- Luke 15:4-7 (NIV): *"Suppose one of you has a hundred sheep and loses one of them. Doesn't he leave the ninety-nine in the open country and go after the lost sheep until he finds it? And when he finds it, he joyfully puts it on his shoulders and goes home."*
- This parable highlights the joy and importance of finding and welcoming back those who are lost.

3. Providing a Safe Haven

In what ways can I help ensure that our community table remains a safe haven for those who feel lost, fostering acceptance, understanding, and a sense of belonging?

The Healing Power of Inclusion

1. Reunion and Restoration

How can I actively participate in creating a space of reunion and restoration for those who feel lost, helping them heal from past wounds and rebuild relationships within our community?

_____
_____
_____
_____
_____

2. The Role of Compassion and Understanding

In what ways can I cultivate compassion and understanding in my interactions with those who feel lost, ensuring they feel safe to express their struggles and know they are valued?

_____
_____
_____
_____
_____

3. Reintegration and Purpose

How can I actively engage those who feel lost in meaningful activities and responsibilities within our community, helping them to rediscover their purpose and sense of belonging?

_____
_____
_____
_____
_____

Scriptural Reference:

- Luke 19:10 (NIV): *"For the Son of Man came to seek and to save the lost."*

- This verse underscores the mission of seeking out and restoring those who are lost, reflecting the compassionate and redemptive nature of the covenant.

Practical Steps for Welcoming the Lost

1. Creating an Inviting Atmosphere

In what ways can I contribute to creating an inviting atmosphere in my community that fosters inclusivity and openness, ensuring that everyone feels welcomed and valued?

_____
_____
_____
_____
_____

2. Offering Support and Guidance

How can I offer meaningful support and guidance to those who are lost, helping them navigate their journey back to the community and ensuring they feel secure and welcomed in their return?

_____
_____
_____
_____
_____

3. Encouraging Active Participation

In what ways can I encourage the lost to actively participate in our community, recognizing and celebrating their contributions to help them feel a genuine sense of belonging and value?

_____
_____
_____
_____
_____

4. Sharing Stories of Redemption

How can I share my own stories of redemption and reconciliation, or those of others, to inspire hope and encourage the lost, while emphasizing the message that everyone is welcomed and valued at God's table?

_____
_____
_____
_____

"The Lost" emphasizes the inclusive and compassionate nature of the covenant of provision, which welcomes those who have strayed or feel disconnected. The table serves as a place of reunion and restoration, offering a safe and accepting space for individuals to reconnect with the community and themselves. By embracing the lost with compassion and understanding, we create an environment where healing and transformation can occur. Let us commit to seeking out and welcoming the lost, recognizing the value of every individual and the importance of offering a place of acceptance and belonging. In doing so, we honor the spirit of the covenant and embody its principles of grace, forgiveness, and unconditional love.

~The Least~

The covenant of provision is a divine promise that extends far beyond the mere distribution of material resources; it embodies a profound commitment to justice, inclusion, and compassion. Central to this covenant is the embrace of "the least"—those who are humble, lowly, or often overlooked by society. These individuals, who may be marginalized due to their socio-economic status, lack of resources, or other circumstances, are too often undervalued in a world that prizes wealth, power, and prestige. Yet, the covenant of provision turns this worldly hierarchy on its head, ensuring that "the least" are not only acknowledged but are offered dignity, respect, and sustenance.

"The least" in this context refers to individuals who find themselves at the margins of society, those who are often invisible in the broader social fabric. They might be the poor, the homeless, the unemployed, or those struggling with physical or mental health issues. They are the individuals who live in the shadows, whose voices are rarely heard, and whose needs are frequently ignored. They are not necessarily the weakest or the least capable, but they are often those who society has pushed aside, failing to recognize their inherent worth.

In many cases, "the least" are people who have been dealt an unfair hand—those born into poverty, those who have faced systemic discrimination, or those who have experienced personal tragedies that have left them vulnerable. Their lives may be marked by a lack of opportunity, a scarcity of resources, or the burden of being undervalued by the very systems that should support them. Yet, it is precisely these individuals whom the covenant of provision seeks to uplift and restore. The covenant of provision is radically inclusive, ensuring that no one is left out—especially not those whom society often overlooks. This covenant recognizes that every person, regardless of their social standing or material wealth, is created in the image of God and possesses intrinsic dignity and worth. It is a covenant that calls for the elevation of "the least," not as an act of charity, but as a fundamental recognition of their humanity.

In the eyes of this covenant, there is no hierarchy of value. The rich and the poor, the powerful and the powerless, the visible and the invisible—all are equally deserving of dignity and sustenance. This is a covenant that rejects the notion that worth is tied to wealth or status. Instead, it affirms that every person has an inherent right to be valued, respected, and provided for.

The sustenance offered by the covenant is not merely about meeting physical needs—though that is certainly a critical component. It is also about restoring dignity to those who have been marginalized. It is about acknowledging the full humanity of "the least" and offering them the same respect and care that is afforded to those who are more privileged. In doing so, the covenant seeks to heal the deep wounds of inequality and exclusion that plague our world.

Inclusion is at the heart of the covenant of provision, and its power to transform lives is profound. When "the least" are included at the table—when they are given not just food, but respect, not just shelter, but dignity—their lives are changed. They are no longer invisible, no longer overlooked. They become full participants in the community, with their contributions recognized and their voices heard.

But the transformation doesn't stop with the individual. When a society embraces "the least," it too is transformed. It becomes a more just, more compassionate community. The act of including "the least" is a reflection of the covenant's broader vision for a world where everyone is valued, where no one is left behind, and where the dignity of every person is upheld.

This inclusion also challenges us to examine our own attitudes and behaviors. It calls us to move beyond mere tolerance or pity and to engage in genuine solidarity with those who are marginalized. It asks us to see "the least" not as objects of charity, but as equal partners in the human family. This is a call to active participation in the covenant's mission, a call to live out the values of justice, compassion, and respect in our daily lives.

The covenant of provision is not just a passive promise; it is a call to action. It challenges us to take concrete steps to elevate "the least" in our communities and in our world. This means advocating for policies that protect the rights of the marginalized, supporting initiatives that provide access to education, healthcare, and employment, and creating spaces where all people are welcomed and valued.

It also means examining our own lives and asking how we can be more inclusive, more compassionate, and more just. How can we ensure that "the least" in our communities are not overlooked or forgotten? How can we extend the covenant's promise of dignity and sustenance to those who need it most?

This call to action is not just for governments or institutions; it is for each of us. It is a call to live out the covenant in our everyday interactions, to be agents of change in our communities, and to work toward a world where every person is valued and every need is met.

The covenant of provision is a powerful declaration of God's love and justice. It is a covenant that embraces "the least" in society, offering them not just sustenance, but dignity and respect. It is a call to action for all of us, challenging us to build a more inclusive and compassionate world.

As we respond to this covenant, we are invited to look beyond the surface, to see the inherent worth in every person, and to work toward a society where no one is overlooked or undervalued. In doing so, we honor the true spirit of the covenant, creating a world where all are included, all are valued, and all are provided for. This is the transformative power of the covenant of provision—a power that can change lives, communities, and ultimately, the world.

The Significance of Honoring "The Least"

1. Recognizing the Marginalized

How can I cultivate a deeper awareness of the struggles faced by marginalized individuals in my community, and in what ways can I actively acknowledge and address the systemic issues that contribute to their challenges?

_____
_____
_____
_____
_____

2. The Call to Justice and Compassion

In what ways can I respond to the call for justice and compassion by advocating for the fair treatment of those in need and challenging societal norms that prioritize the powerful, and how can I actively uplift individuals who may feel marginalized or overlooked?

_____
_____

_____
_____
_____

Scriptural Reference:

- Matthew 25:40 (NIV): *"The King will reply, 'Truly I tell you, whatever you did for one of the least of these brothers and sisters of mine, you did for me.'"*
- This verse underscores the importance of caring for the least, equating acts of kindness and support for them with serving the divine.

3. Offering Dignity and Respect

How can I honor the dignity and humanity of those who are marginalized in my community by actively listening to their stories and valuing their experiences, and in what ways can I help foster a culture of respect and affirmation?

_____
_____
_____
_____

The Covenant's Commitment to Providing Sustenance

1. Meeting Basic Needs

In what ways can I actively contribute to meeting the basic needs of those in my community, ensuring they have access to food, shelter, and healthcare, and how does this commitment reflect the principles of justice and equity in my faith?

_____
_____
_____
_____

2. Empowerment and Support

How can I participate in empowering individuals from marginalized communities by providing opportunities for education and personal development, and in what ways can I support initiatives that help them build the skills needed to thrive?

_____
_____
_____
_____
_____

3. Creating Inclusive Communities

In what ways can I actively contribute to creating inclusive communities that value and support everyone, especially those who are marginalized, and how can I help break down barriers that hinder their full participation?

_____
_____
_____
_____
_____

Scriptural Reference:

- Proverbs 31:8-9 (NIV): *"Speak up for those who cannot speak for themselves, for the rights of all who are destitute. Speak up and judge fairly; defend the rights of the poor and needy."*
- This passage calls for advocacy and defense of the rights of the marginalized, highlighting the covenant's commitment to justice.

Practical Steps for Supporting "The Least"
1. Advocacy and Awareness

How can I raise awareness about the challenges faced by marginalized individuals in my community, and in what ways can I advocate for policies that promote their rights and well-being?

_____
_____
_____
_____

2. Providing Direct Support

In what ways can I engage in direct support activities to assist those in need within my community, and how can I encourage others to join me in making a meaningful impact through volunteering or donating resources?

_____
_____
_____
_____

3. Building Relationships

How can I intentionally build relationships with those who are often marginalized or overlooked, and what steps can I take to listen to their stories, understand their needs, and offer meaningful support?

_____
_____
_____
_____

4. Promoting Inclusive Practices

In what ways can I actively promote inclusive practices in my community or workplace, ensuring that everyone has equal access to opportunities and feels valued and welcomed?

_____

_____

_____

_____

_____

"The Least" emphasizes the covenant's commitment to embracing and supporting those who are humble, lowly, or marginalized. By offering dignity and sustenance, the covenant challenges societal norms and advocates for justice, compassion, and inclusion. Supporting the least is not just an act of charity but a moral and spiritual obligation that reflects the values of the covenant. Let us strive to honor and uplift the least, recognizing their inherent worth and working to create a more just and equitable society. In doing so, we embody the principles of the covenant and contribute to a community where everyone can thrive.

~Food Fights~

An absolute disastrous mess! That's probably the best way to describe the scene at the "Choice" Buffet Restaurant, a popular spot in my hometown back in the '90s. My brother Walter, my cousin Antoine, our friend Karl, and I were regulars there, enjoying all the fried chicken and soft-serve ice cream our hearts desired. But one day, things took a turn for the chaotic. We got into a squabble with some folks at a nearby table—over what, I can't even remember—and before you knew it, mashed potatoes were flying, and chicken wings were soaring through the air. What started as a simple disagreement turned into a full-blown food fight, and let's just say we got kicked out faster than you can say "buffet."

Now, food fights—whether they involve actual spaghetti flying across the room or just heated words—have a funny way of turning even the most peaceful places into battlegrounds. The dining table, a place where people are supposed to come together, share a meal, and enjoy each other's company, can quickly become the setting for conflict when tensions rise. It's meant to be a space of unity, where relationships are strengthened over a good meal. But when disagreements pop up—

whether over the last slice of pizza, differing opinions, or underlying personal issues—that harmony can quickly dissolve into chaos.

It's a reminder that even the places where we gather for nourishment and connection aren't immune to conflict. But here's the thing: just as quickly as a table can become a battleground, it can also become a place of reconciliation and understanding. It all depends on how we handle the moments when tensions bubble up. Because let's face it, life's too short to waste on food fights—whether they're literal or metaphorical. In the context of the covenant of provision, such conflicts stand in stark contrast to the principles of community, sharing, and respect that are at the heart of this covenant. The covenant of provision is not merely about ensuring that everyone has enough to eat; it is also about fostering a spirit of unity and mutual respect. It calls on us to resolve conflicts peacefully, to maintain harmony, and to create an environment where everyone feels valued and respected.

The table is a powerful symbol of community and togetherness. Throughout history, sharing a meal has been a universal act of fellowship, a moment where barriers are broken down and connections are strengthened. In many cultures, the table is seen as a sacred space where families and communities come together to celebrate, to support one another, and to find solace in each other's company.

However, when conflicts arise at the table, this sacred space can be easily disrupted. A literal food fight may involve throwing physical objects, but a metaphorical food fight—such as harsh words, unresolved tensions, or competitive attitudes—can be just as damaging. These conflicts can turn a place meant for unity into one of division, where the focus shifts from sharing and understanding to winning and losing.

The covenant of provision, which emphasizes the values of sharing, respect, and community, challenges us to approach conflicts with a spirit of reconciliation rather than confrontation. This covenant invites us to view the table not as a place where differences must be settled through argument or force, but as a place where understanding and compromise can be achieved.

In practical terms, this means that when conflicts arise, whether at the dining table or in broader contexts, we are called to seek peaceful resolutions. This involves active listening, empathy, and a willingness to put the needs of the community above personal pride or grievances. It means recognizing that every person at the table has a voice that deserves to be heard and a perspective that deserves to be respected. Moreover, the covenant of provision reminds us that maintaining harmony is not just about avoiding conflict but about actively fostering a sense of unity. This may involve making space for difficult conversations, addressing underlying issues that may be causing tension, and working together to find solutions that honor the dignity and needs of everyone involved.

Harmony is essential to the well-being of any community. Just as a meal is more enjoyable when everyone at the table is at peace with one another, a community thrives when its members are united in purpose and mutual respect. Conflicts, when left unresolved, can fester and grow, leading to divisions that undermine the very fabric of the community. They can create an atmosphere of distrust and resentment, making it difficult for people to come together and work toward common goals.

The covenant of provision calls on us to be stewards not only of the physical resources we share but also of the relationships that bind us together. It urges us to be proactive in maintaining harmony, to address conflicts with humility and grace, and to strive for resolutions that strengthen rather than weaken the bonds of community.

This commitment to harmony reflects a deeper understanding of the covenant's values. It recognizes that true provision is not just about meeting material needs but also about nurturing the emotional and spiritual well-being of the community. When we resolve conflicts with compassion and respect, we honor the covenant and contribute to the creation of a more just and loving society.

Conflicts, while challenging, also present opportunities for growth and deeper understanding. When approached with the right mindset, conflicts can lead to stronger relationships and a more cohesive community. The covenant of provision encourages us to see conflicts not as threats but as chances to learn from one another, to grow in empathy, and to find creative solutions that benefit everyone.

By engaging in constructive dialogue, we can transform moments of tension into opportunities for building trust and deepening our connections with others. This process requires patience, openness, and a commitment to the principles of the covenant—principles that prioritize the well-being of the community over individual desires.

The covenant of provision is a powerful reminder of our responsibility to foster unity and respect within our communities. Whether at the dining table or in the broader context of our lives, we are called to resolve conflicts with wisdom and compassion, to maintain harmony, and to ensure that our actions reflect the values of the covenant.

In doing so, we not only honor the spirit of the covenant but also contribute to the creation of a world where everyone is valued, where differences are respected, and where conflicts are resolved in ways that strengthen rather than divide. This is the true essence of the covenant of provision—a commitment to building a community where peace, justice, and love prevail as opposed to the current tribalism that encourages scoring political points and attempting to rub our being 'right" or our "winnings" in other's face.

Understanding Conflicts at the Table
   1. Sources of Conflict
   What sources of conflict do I notice in my own relationships or community gatherings, and how can I approach these differences with a spirit of understanding and reconciliation to promote harmony and unity?

   _____
   _____
   _____
   _____

2. The Impact of Unresolved Conflicts

What steps can I take to address and resolve any unresolved conflicts in my life to foster a sense of community and belonging at the table, ensuring that I contribute to an atmosphere of comfort, unity, and open communication?

_____
_____
_____
_____
_____

3. The Symbolism of the Table

In what ways can I honor the symbolism of the table in my life, fostering unity and nourishment in my relationships, and how can I address conflicts that arise to ensure that the table remains a space of harmony and respect?

_____
_____
_____
_____
_____

The Importance of Resolving Conflicts

1. Upholding the Spirit of the Covenant

How can I actively uphold the spirit of the covenant in my interactions with others, and what steps can I take to resolve conflicts in a way that promotes generosity, respect, and inclusivity?

_____
_____
_____
_____
_____

Scriptural Reference:

- Matthew 5:23-24 (NIV): *"Therefore, if you are offering your gift at the altar and there remember that your brother or sister has something against you, leave your gift there in front of the altar. First go and be reconciled to them; then come and offer your gift."*
- This passage emphasizes the importance of reconciliation and resolving conflicts, even before engaging in sacred rituals.

2. Fostering Healthy Communication
In what ways can I foster healthy communication in my relationships, and how can I create an environment where everyone feels safe to express their feelings and concerns?

_____
_____
_____
_____
_____

3. Promoting a Positive and Inclusive Environment
How can I contribute to creating a positive and inclusive environment in my community, and what steps can I take to ensure that everyone feels safe, respected, and valued?

_____
_____
_____
_____
_____

Strategies for Resolving Conflicts and Maintaining Harmony

1. Open Communication and Active Listening
In what ways can I foster open communication in my relationships, and how might practicing active listening deepen my understanding of others and prevent misunderstandings?

_____
_____

2. Practicing Empathy and Understanding

How can I cultivate empathy in my interactions with others, and in what specific ways might understanding their perspectives help me approach conflicts with compassion and foster more constructive conversations?

3. Finding Common Ground

In what ways can I actively seek to identify shared goals or values in my relationships, and how can focusing on our common ground help transform conflicts into opportunities for collaboration and understanding?

4. Setting Boundaries and Expectations

What steps can I take to clearly communicate my boundaries and expectations in my relationships, and how might doing so help prevent conflicts and foster healthier interactions both at the table and in my daily life?

5. Seeking Mediation or Facilitation

How can I be open to seeking mediation or facilitation when faced with challenging conflicts, and in what ways might involving a neutral third party help me and others find common ground and mutually agreeable solutions?

6. Practicing Forgiveness and Letting Go

In what ways can I practice forgiveness in my own life, letting go of grudges and resentment, and how can this act of letting go help me restore relationships and move forward positively?

"Food Fights" highlights the reality that conflicts can arise even in settings intended for unity and sharing, such as the dining table. The close proximity and intimacy often experienced at the table can sometimes intensify these conflicts. However, God's covenant emphasizes the importance of resolving these conflicts to maintain harmony and uphold the values of generosity, respect, and inclusivity. By practicing open communication, empathy, and forgiveness, we can navigate conflicts constructively and foster a positive, welcoming environment. Let us commit to resolving conflicts with compassion and understanding, ensuring that the table remains a place of unity, nourishment, and shared experiences for all.

~Crumbs from the Table: Lessons from the Leftovers~

The phrase "getting the crumbs from the table" often conjures images of scarcity and lack, but beneath this image lies a profound lesson in humility, gratitude, and resourcefulness. It invites us to rethink our perspectives on what is valuable and to recognize that even the smallest, seemingly insignificant pieces of life can hold great worth.

At its core, "getting the crumbs from the table" is a lesson in humility. It challenges us to reconsider our expectations and entitlements. In a world that often prizes abundance and excess, we can become blind to the value of the small and the overlooked. This metaphor calls us to a posture of humility, where we learn to appreciate even the modest portions that life offers us.

Humility doesn't mean settling for less or denying our worth; rather, it is an acknowledgment that life's true value isn't always found in grandeur but in the everyday, often overlooked moments. It teaches us to see the beauty in simplicity, to find contentment in what we have, no matter how small it may seem. By embracing the "crumbs" with humility, we open ourselves to a deeper understanding of what it means to be truly rich—not in material wealth, but in spirit and heart.

Gratitude is the natural companion to humility. When we learn to be grateful for the crumbs, we begin to see the world through a lens of abundance rather than scarcity. What might initially seem insignificant—a kind word, a small gesture, a simple meal—can become a source of immense value when viewed with a grateful heart.

"Getting the crumbs from the table" reminds us that every blessing, no matter how small, is a gift worth cherishing. It encourages us to cultivate a mindset of gratitude, where we recognize the worth of the everyday blessings that might otherwise go unnoticed. This gratitude transforms our lives, allowing us to find joy and satisfaction in what we have, rather than constantly yearning for more.

In the story of the Syrophoenician woman in the Gospels, we see a powerful example of this attitude. She asks for nothing more than the crumbs from the table, demonstrating a faith and gratitude that ultimately leads to her receiving far more than she requested. Her story is a testament to the transformative power of gratitude, showing that even the smallest blessings can lead to great outcomes when received with a thankful heart.

Beyond humility and gratitude, the concept of "getting the crumbs from the table" also teaches us about resourcefulness. Life does not always provide us with abundance in the ways we might expect, but that doesn't mean we are without resources. This metaphor encourages us to make the most of what we have, to see potential where others might see waste, and to use every bit of what is available to us.

Resourcefulness is the ability to see possibilities where others see limitations. It's about being creative, innovative, and wise in the way we use our resources—no matter how small they may seem. Those who have learned to make the most of the crumbs often discover that they can accomplish much with little. This approach not only maximizes the utility of what we have but also fosters a sense of empowerment, as we learn to rely on our ingenuity and resilience.

In this way, the crumbs from the table become not just leftovers, but the starting point for something greater. They represent the opportunities that exist within the constraints of our circumstances, the potential for growth and success even in the face of adversity.

The metaphor of "getting the crumbs from the table" can be applied to various aspects of life, from our personal relationships to our professional endeavors. It challenges us to find value in the small interactions that build relationships, in the incremental steps that lead to success, and in the minor victories that contribute to a fulfilling life.

In our relationships, it might mean appreciating the small acts of kindness and love that often go unnoticed but are the true building blocks of lasting connections. In our work, it might mean recognizing the importance of small achievements and using them as stepping stones to greater accomplishments. In our spiritual lives, it might mean finding meaning in the everyday moments of grace that draw us closer to a deeper understanding of our purpose.

This mindset also has profound implications for how we view others. It encourages us to see the value in every person, even those who might be marginalized or overlooked by society. It reminds us that every individual, no matter how small their role may appear, contributes to the richness of our shared human experience.

The concept of "getting the crumbs from the table" is a powerful metaphor that teaches us essential life lessons in humility, gratitude, and resourcefulness. It reminds us that true richness is not always found in abundance but in the ability to appreciate and make the most of what we have, however small it may seem.

By embracing this mindset, we learn to find value in the overlooked, to be grateful for the small blessings, and to use every resource at our disposal to its fullest potential. In doing so, we cultivate a life that is not only rich in material terms but also rich in spirit, connection, and meaning. The crumbs from the table, far from being insignificant, become symbols of the hidden riches that life offers to those who are willing to see and appreciate them.

1. Value in the Small Things
How can I cultivate a mindset that values and appreciates the small blessings in my life, recognizing that even the tiniest resources can hold significant value, and what steps can I take to be more mindful and grateful for what I have?

_____
_____
_____
_____
_____

2. Humility and Acceptance
In what areas of my life do I need to practice humility and acceptance, recognizing that not everyone receives the same

portions, and how can this perspective help me cultivate empathy and understanding for others who may have less?

___

3. Resourcefulness and Innovation
How can I cultivate a mindset of resourcefulness and innovation in my life, seeing the potential in what may seem like leftovers or wasted opportunities, and what creative ways can I transform them into something valuable?

___

4. Gratitude and Contentment
In what ways can I practice gratitude for the small blessings in my life, and how might this shift in focus from what I lack to what I have foster a deeper sense of contentment and joy?

___

5. Spiritual and Moral Lessons
What can I learn from the story of the Canaanite woman about faith and humility, and how can I seek and recognize the small blessings in my life as powerful acts of God's grace?

___

6. Inclusion and Equity

How can I actively work towards greater inclusion and equity in my community, ensuring that all individuals have access to the resources they need to thrive, rather than merely settling for the leftovers?

7. Sustainability and Stewardship

In what ways can I practice sustainability and stewardship in my daily life, ensuring that I make efficient use of the resources God has provided while also contributing to a more just and sustainable world?

"Getting the crumbs from the table" offers rich lessons in humility, resourcefulness, gratitude, and social responsibility. It challenges us to appreciate the small things, to be innovative with limited resources, and to strive for a more inclusive and equitable society. By embracing these lessons, we can cultivate a deeper sense of purpose and fulfillment in our lives, finding value in every experience and resource available to us even when on surface it appears we lack. Crumbs, 2 fish, five loaves of bread are our reminder that God has stretching power, and miraculous, always ensures there's enough.

~Flipping Tables: A Call to Advocate for Justice~

The phrase "flipping tables" has come to symbolize moments of righteous indignation, often evoking the powerful image of Jesus overturning the tables of the money changers in the Temple. This dramatic act, recorded in the Gospels, is far more than an outburst of anger; it is a profound and deliberate demonstration of the pursuit of justice and integrity, particularly within a sacred space. It challenges us to reflect on the importance of standing against corruption and injustice wherever they are found. In the words of Charles Darwin, *"If the misery of the poor be caused not by the laws of nature, but by our institutions, great is our sin."* In such cases, tables need to be flipped!

When Jesus flipped the tables in the Temple, it was a bold and symbolic act aimed at confronting the exploitation and greed that had infiltrated a place meant to be holy and sacred. The Temple, which was supposed to be a house of prayer for all nations, had become a marketplace where the poor were marginalized and the sacred was commodified. Jesus' actions were a clear and unambiguous rejection of this corruption—a call to restore the true purpose of the Temple as a place of worship and community, free from the taint of exploitation.

This act of flipping tables is not merely about anger; it is about the deep moral outrage that arises when sacred spaces and principles are violated. It is a call to action for all who witness injustice, urging them not to remain silent or passive but to take a stand, even when it requires bold and uncomfortable actions. It reminds us that there are times when advocating for justice necessitates disruption—when overturning the status quo is necessary to restore what is right and just.

However, as Caleb Campbell wisely observes, *"Jesus certainly did flip tables, but he set exponentially more tables than he flipped."* This statement underscores a crucial aspect of Jesus' ministry: while there are moments that require bold actions to confront injustice, the broader mission is one of healing, restoration, and inclusivity. Jesus' primary work was not about destruction but about creation—creating spaces of welcome, community, and love where all could gather and be nourished.

The act of setting tables is a metaphor for the continuous work of building relationships, fostering understanding, and creating environments where justice, compassion, and integrity can flourish. While flipping tables is sometimes necessary to clear out the corruption and make way for justice, the ultimate goal is to set tables where all are invited, where peace and righteousness reign, and where the dignity of every person is honored.

This balance between flipping tables and setting them is vital. It teaches us that the pursuit of justice must be coupled with the pursuit of peace. While we must be unafraid to confront wrongdoing and injustice, we must also be equally committed to building and nurturing communities where equity and love are the guiding principles.

The story of Jesus flipping tables in the Temple serves as a timeless reminder of the responsibility to advocate for justice, especially when faced with systemic wrongdoing. It calls us to be vigilant in protecting what is sacred, whether that is a physical space, a community, or a principle. It challenges us to confront systems and practices that exploit the vulnerable and to demand integrity in the places and institutions that are meant to serve the common good.

At the same time, it calls us to be builders and restorers. After the tables have been overturned, after the corruption has been exposed and dismantled, the work of setting the table begins—creating spaces where people can come together, where healing can occur, and where justice is not just a concept but a lived reality.

This dual call to flip tables when necessary and to set tables whenever possible is a powerful framework for how we engage with the world around us. It teaches us that advocacy for justice is not only about resistance but also about creation—creating new ways of living and relating that reflect the values of fairness, compassion, and respect for all.

"Flipping tables" is a potent symbol of the fight against injustice, reminding us that there are moments when bold, disruptive action is required to correct what is wrong. But this is only one part of the mission. The greater work is found in setting tables—in building and sustaining communities where justice and compassion prevail.

As we reflect on the actions of Jesus in the Temple, we are reminded of the importance of both aspects of this mission. We must be willing to confront and overturn the systems of injustice that harm and exploit, but we must also be dedicated to the ongoing work of creating spaces where all are valued, where peace and justice are the foundation, and where love guides our actions.

In this way, the act of flipping tables and the act of setting them become two sides of the same coin—a unified mission that calls us to advocate for justice in all its forms, to stand against what is wrong, and to work tirelessly to build what is right.

1. The Context of the Event

The incident, described in the Gospels (Matthew 21:12-13, Mark 11:15-18, Luke 19:45-46, and John 2:13-16), occurs during the Passover festival. The Temple in Jerusalem was a central place for worship and sacrifice, attracting pilgrims from all over. However, the outer courts of the Temple had become a marketplace where merchants and money changers operated, often exploiting worshippers by charging exorbitant rates for the exchange of foreign currency and the sale of sacrificial animals.

_____
_____
_____
_____
_____

2. Jesus' Actions and Words

Jesus' reaction—overturning the tables and driving out the merchants—was a direct challenge to the corruption and exploitation occurring in a place meant for worship and prayer. He declared, "It is written, *'My house shall be called a house of prayer,'* but you make it a den of robbers" (Matthew 21:13).

3. Advocating for Justice

Challenging Exploitation and Corruption: By disrupting the commercial activities, Jesus was standing against the exploitation of the poor and the distortion of religious practices for profit. His actions underscored the importance of justice and fairness, particularly in religious and spiritual contexts.

- Restoring Sacredness: Jesus' actions were also about restoring the true purpose of the Temple as a place of worship and communion with God. By advocating for a return to the core values of faith, he highlighted the need for integrity and purity in religious practices. How can I actively work to restore the sacredness of my own worship practices and community, ensuring that my faith reflects integrity and genuine communion with God?

- A Call to Righteous Anger: The incident shows that righteous anger—anger directed at injustice and wrongdoing—can be a powerful force for good. It serves as a reminder that standing up against oppression and exploitation is a critical aspect of advocating for justice. In what ways does the example of righteous anger inspire me to stand up against injustice in my own life, and how can I channel that anger into meaningful action for the good of others?

_____
_____
_____
_____
_____

4. Contemporary Implications

The "flipping tables" event can inspire modern-day advocates for justice to take bold actions against systemic injustices. It encourages people to:

- Confront Injustice: Be willing to speak out and act against corruption, exploitation, and inequality, even when it means challenging established systems. How can I live this out?

- Promote Fairness and Integrity: Strive to uphold ethical standards in all areas of life, including business, religion, and politics. How can I live this out?

___

- Empower the Marginalized: Like Jesus' concern for those being exploited, advocacy should focus on protecting and empowering the vulnerable and marginalized in society. How can I live this out?

___

In summary, "flipping tables" symbolizes a strong stand against injustice and the commitment to restoring fairness and integrity. It reminds us that advocating for justice sometimes requires bold, decisive actions that challenge the status quo and address deep-rooted issues of exploitation and corruption.

Chapter 6
The Coming Feast

While the hunger we feel for peace, unity, justice, and the restoration of kindness is profound, it is often hard to imagine a world where these virtues are the norm rather than the exception. In our current reality, these are rare delicacies, seldom found on the tables we gather around. Instead, we are too often served dishes of division, discord, and injustice—leaving us longing for something better, something more nourishing to our souls.

Yet, even in the midst of this scarcity, there is a hope that burns brightly—a promise that there is a feast coming where these elusive dishes will be served in abundance. This is not just wishful thinking or an idealistic dream; it is a profound and urgent truth rooted in the deepest promises of our faith. The hunger we feel for peace, unity, justice, and kindness is not in vain; it is a sign of the greater meal that is being prepared for us.

This coming feast is not just a metaphor; it is a future reality that has been foretold, a banquet where the table is set with everything our hearts long for. Peace will not be a rare garnish but the main course, served generously to all who gather. Unity will no longer be a fleeting taste but a staple that nourishes every conversation and every relationship. Justice will not be an occasional side dish but the bread that sustains and strengthens us. And kindness—oh, kindness—will be the sweet, overflowing cup that never runs dry.

This feast is the fulfillment of every promise made by the Provider, a feast that will satisfy every deep hunger we have carried through this broken world. It is the assurance that the day is coming when the divisions that tear us apart will be healed, when the injustices that plague us will be righted, and when the harshness that wearies our spirits will be replaced with the soft embrace of kindness.

But this promise is not just for a distant future; it has implications for how we live right now. While we wait for that feast, we are called to prepare for it by cultivating these virtues in our own lives and communities. We are invited to set our own tables with as much peace, unity, justice, and kindness as we can muster, even in a world that often seems starved for them. In doing so, we become a foretaste of the feast to come, giving those around us a glimpse of the abundance that is promised.

The urgency of this calling cannot be overstated. The world is hungry—desperately so—and we, who know of the coming feast, have a responsibility to share what we have, to make room at our tables for others, and to serve up as much of these life-giving dishes as possible. We cannot be content with waiting; we must act with the hope that fuels our hearts, knowing that every act of peace, every gesture of unity, every fight for justice, and every word of kindness is not wasted but is a preparation for that greater meal.

And so, while the hunger for these virtues is intense and the vision of their abundance might seem distant, we can live with the confident hope that the feast is coming. A feast where the table will overflow with everything we have longed for and more. A feast where every hunger will be satisfied, every longing fulfilled, and every tear wiped away. Until that day arrives, we work, we wait, and we hope—knowing that the Provider's promise is sure, and the banquet of peace, unity, justice, and kindness is not just a dream, but a coming reality.

The urgency of this hope compels us to act, even in the face of overwhelming odds. We live in a world where the hunger for peace is palpable, where the cries for justice echo in every corner, and where the longing for unity and kindness seems almost desperate. In such a world, it's easy to feel discouraged, to wonder if our small efforts can really make a difference. But it's precisely in these moments of doubt that we must cling to the promise of the coming feast, a promise that assures us our work is not in vain.

Every time we choose peace over conflict, every time we extend a hand of reconciliation, we are setting the table for that future banquet. Every time we stand up for justice, refusing to turn a blind eye to the suffering of others, we are laying the foundation for the feast where justice will reign. Every time we build bridges instead of walls, fostering unity in a world that thrives on division, we are preparing for the day when all will be one. And every act of kindness, no matter how small, is a taste of the sweet abundance that awaits us.

The promise of the coming feast also challenges us to reimagine our present reality. It pushes us to see beyond the scarcity that dominates our world, to envision a future where abundance is the norm. This vision of abundance isn't just about material wealth; it's about the richness of relationships, the depth of community, and the overflowing of love and grace. It's about creating spaces where everyone is welcome, where no one goes hungry—physically, spiritually, or emotionally—and where the table is always expanding to include more people, more stories, more lives.

But this vision requires more than just hope; it requires action. We are called to be both dreamers and doers, to hold the vision of the coming feast in one hand and the tools for building it in the other. This means being intentional about how we live, how we interact with others, and how we use our resources. It means prioritizing the values of peace, unity, justice, and kindness in our daily lives, even when it's difficult, even when it costs us something. Because every decision we make, every action we take, can either contribute to the hunger of the world or help satisfy it.

As we work towards this vision, we must also remember that we are not alone. The promise of the coming feast is not just an individual hope; it's a communal one. We are part of a larger story, a story that stretches back through generations of people who have hungered and thirsted for the same things we do. We stand on the shoulders of those who came before us, who fought for peace, who demanded justice, who built unity in the face of division, and who spread kindness in a world that often lacked it. And we are joined by countless others around the world today, all working towards the same vision, all contributing to the same feast.

This collective effort gives us strength, reminding us that even when our individual efforts seem small, together they add up to something powerful. Together, we are setting the table for the feast that is to come, preparing a place where peace, unity, justice, and kindness are not just occasional dishes but the main course. And as we do this, we create glimpses of that future in the present, offering the world a taste of what is possible.

In the end, the hunger we feel for these virtues is not a sign of despair but a sign of hope. It's a reminder that we were created for more than what we see around us, that we were made for a world where abundance is the rule and not the exception. The coming feast is not just a promise for the future; it's a call to action in the present. It invites us to live as though the feast has already begun, to bring as much of that future reality into our world today as we can.

So, as we wait for the day when we shall never hunger or thirst again, let us be the ones who feed the world with peace, who quench the thirst for justice, who serve up unity, and who sprinkle kindness liberally over everything we do. Let us live in such a way that when the feast finally arrives, we'll recognize it—not just because we've dreamed of it, but because we've already been working to set the table. And in that moment, we'll see that every effort, every sacrifice, every act of love was worth it, as we join together in the ultimate celebration of all that is good, true, and beautiful.

~The Last Supper~

Can you imagine being an invited to a dinner that would not only go down in history but also change the course of humanity forever? That's exactly what happened at the Last Supper—a meal that wasn't just any ordinary get-together but a profound moment that laid the foundation for one of the most significant events in Christian tradition. The Last Supper is more than just a famous painting by Leonardo da Vinci; it's a powerful illustration of the covenant of provision, where Jesus shared his final meal with his disciples before his crucifixion, instituted the Eucharist, and introduced the new covenant that would reshape the relationship between God and humanity.

Picture this: Jesus and his twelve disciples are gathered around the table, sharing a meal. But this isn't just any meal—it's Passover, a time already rich with symbolism and tradition. You can almost hear the clinking of cups, the breaking of bread, and the murmurs of conversation. Yet, beneath the surface of this seemingly ordinary meal, something extraordinary is unfolding. Jesus, fully aware of the events about to transpire, uses this moment to leave a lasting legacy, not only in words but in actions that would echo through the ages.

Here, Jesus doesn't just pass around the bread and wine; he gives them new meaning. The bread becomes his body, broken for the salvation of humanity, and the wine becomes his blood, poured out as a new covenant between God and his people. It's as if he's saying, "This meal is more than just sustenance for your bodies—it's sustenance for your souls."

The Last Supper is the ultimate illustration of the covenant of provision. In this moment, Jesus doesn't just provide food; he provides himself. He takes the everyday elements of bread and wine—things his disciples were familiar with—and transforms them into symbols of a deeper spiritual reality. This act of sharing is about more than filling stomachs; it's about filling lives with grace, forgiveness, and the promise of eternal life.

Jesus knew that the path ahead would be difficult, not just for himself but for his disciples and all who would follow him. So, he offered them—and us—a way to stay connected, to remember, and to be sustained. The Last Supper is a reminder that even in the face of suffering, God's provision is abundant, and his covenant is unbreakable.

The Last Supper wasn't just a farewell dinner; it was a moment of teaching and revelation. Jesus used this opportunity to speak to his disciples about what was to come—his impending sacrifice and the establishment of a new covenant. He knew this would be hard for them to understand, so he gave them something tangible to hold onto. Every time they would break bread or drink wine, they would remember this night, this meal, and the promises made.

But let's not forget the very human aspect of this meal. These were men who had spent years together, sharing countless meals, stories, and experiences. They were friends, teachers, and students. The Last Supper was a moment of profound connection, where Jesus offered not just spiritual truths but also the comfort of shared humanity. He acknowledged their fears and uncertainties, providing them with the strength they would need to carry on after he was gone.

While the Last Supper is a moment of reflection and remembrance, it's also a call to action. Jesus didn't just institute the Eucharist as a ritual to be observed; he called his followers to live out the meaning of that ritual in their daily lives. "Do this in remembrance of me," he said—not just the act of breaking bread and sharing wine, but the act of living in a way that reflects the love, sacrifice, and grace that these symbols represent.

This meal is a powerful reminder that we are called to be a people of provision, just as God provides for us. We are called to share what we have—whether it's food, time, love, or resources—with those around us, especially with those in need. The Last Supper challenges us to look beyond our own needs and to see the needs of others, to be the hands and feet of Christ in the world.

The Last Supper is more than just a historical event; it's a meal that continues to nourish and inspire. Every time we participate in the Eucharist, we are drawn into that upper room, joining Jesus and his disciples at the table. We are reminded of the covenant of provision, the promise that God will always provide for us, even in the darkest of times.

This meal, this moment, is a profound invitation to live out the values that Jesus embodied—love, sacrifice, humility, and service. It's a reminder that we are part of a larger story, a story that began at a table with twelve disciples and continues to unfold in our lives today.

So, the next time you think of the Last Supper, remember that it's not just about the past—it's about the present and the future. It's about the ongoing invitation to share in God's provision and to be a source of provision for others. It's a meal that changed everything and continues to change us, one bite, one sip, one act of love at a time.

The Significance of the Last Supper

1. The Establishment of the New Covenant

How does the establishment of the new covenant at the Last Supper shape my understanding of redemption and reconciliation, and in what ways can I embody this covenant in my daily life?

_____
_____
_____
_____
_____

Scriptural Reference:

- Luke 22:19-20 (NIV): "And he took bread, gave thanks and broke it, and gave it to them, saying, 'This is my body given for you; do this in remembrance of me.' In the same way, after the supper he took the cup, saying, 'This cup is the new covenant in my blood, which is poured out for you.'"
- This passage highlights the establishment of the new covenant, marked by Jesus's impending sacrifice.

2. A Symbol of Sacrificial Love

In what ways does the sacrificial love demonstrated by Jesus at the Last Supper challenge me to reflect on my own relationships and call me to act with greater love and selflessness towards others?

_____
_____
_____
_____
_____

3. The Eucharist and Its Meaning

How does participating in the Eucharist deepen my understanding of Jesus's love and sacrifice, and in what ways can I reflect that unity with fellow believers in my daily life?

_____
_____
_____
_____
_____

4. A Message of Unity and Fellowship

In what ways does the Last Supper inspire me to cultivate unity and fellowship within my community, and how can I actively promote love and mutual support among fellow believers as a reflection of our shared faith?

_____
_____
_____
_____
_____

5. The Promise of Eternal Life

How does the promise of eternal life, as revealed in the Last Supper, shape my understanding of communion with God, and in what ways can I live today in anticipation of sharing in that divine banquet?

_____
_____
_____
_____
_____

Scriptural Reference:

- John 6:54 (NIV): *"Whoever eats my flesh and drinks my blood has eternal life, and I will raise them up at the last day."*

The Table Book   Jermaine E. Pennington

- This verse connects the act of partaking in the Eucharist with the promise of eternal life.

The Last Supper's Message for Believers

1. Reflecting on Sacrificial Love

In what ways can I actively reflect on and emulate the sacrificial love of Jesus demonstrated at the Last Supper in my daily relationships, ensuring that I prioritize the needs of others with selflessness and compassion?

_____
_____
_____
_____
_____

2. Embracing the New Covenant

How can I more fully embrace the new covenant established at the Last Supper, allowing God's forgiveness and grace to transform my relationship with Him and guide my actions towards others?

_____
_____
_____
_____
_____

3. Fostering Unity and Community

In what ways does the communal aspect of the Last Supper challenge me to foster unity and support within my church community, and how can I actively nurture relationships that reflect the love and harmony of Christ?

_____
_____
_____

4. Anticipating the Fulfillment of the Kingdom

How does the anticipation of the fulfillment of God's kingdom, as reflected in the Last Supper, inspire me to remain steadfast in my faith journey, and in what practical ways can I cultivate hope and expectation for eternal life in my daily life?

The Last Supper is a profound and multifaceted event that encapsulates the essence of the covenant of provision. It highlights themes of sacrificial love, unity, and eternal promise, offering a powerful message for believers. As a central element of Christian faith, the Last Supper calls believers to remember Jesus's sacrifice, embrace the new covenant, and live in unity and love with one another. It also provides a hopeful vision of the future, where the promises of the covenant will be fully realized in eternal communion with God. Let us, therefore, reflect on the significance of the Last Supper and strive to embody its teachings in our daily lives.

Through this sacred meal, we are reminded of God's unwavering commitment to His people and the lengths to which He has gone to restore us to Himself. The breaking of bread and sharing of the cup symbolize not only Jesus's body and blood but also the profound generosity and grace that are at the heart of God's relationship with humanity. As we partake in this holy remembrance, we are invited to enter into a deeper understanding of God's love, to extend that same love to others, and to live as people who are continually shaped by the covenant's call to mercy, compassion, and faithful service. In doing so, we keep alive the spirit of the Last Supper, allowing it to transform our hearts and guide us on our journey toward a fuller communion with God and one another.

~Communion as a Foretaste~

I recently came across a sign that said, *"Having imaginary friends is strange, but pretending to eat them and drink their blood is crazy."* This was a clear jab at Christianity and the sacred act of Communion. But this critique isn't new. The Romans once accused early Christians of cannibalism, completely misunderstanding what Communion and the Christian faith are truly about.

Communion is much more than a ritual—it's an invitation to the most significant meal of our lives. Yet, instead of receiving a beautifully worded invitation, we're given a taste—a small, sacred morsel that hints at the extraordinary feast that awaits us. This is the true essence of Communion. It's not just a church tradition or a routine practice; it's a divine preview, a profound glimpse of the ultimate celebration in God's kingdom.

Communion transcends the physical elements of bread and wine (or juice, depending on your tradition). It's not merely about taking a sip or a bite; it's about embracing a profound promise—a covenant of provision, a guarantee that God will sustain us now and forever.

But Communion isn't just about remembering what has been done; it's about looking forward to what is yet to come. When you hold that small piece of bread and that tiny cup, you are holding onto the essence of hope itself. It's a foretaste, a sign of the greater fulfillment that is on its way.

Who doesn't love a truly great meal—the kind that leaves you eagerly anticipating the next course even before you've finished the first? Communion is that first taste, sparking our anticipation and reminding us that what's coming is beyond anything we can imagine. It's a foretaste of the ultimate banquet, where every seat is filled, every dish is perfect, and all are welcome.

This feast we anticipate isn't just any meal—it's the final fulfillment of God's Kingdom. When we partake in Communion, we're not simply eating bread or drinking wine; we're experiencing a glimpse of a future

The Table Book   Jermaine E. Pennington

where all that is broken is restored, where every tear is wiped away, and where love and justice reign supreme. It's like receiving a VIP pass to the most extraordinary event ever, with the joy of knowing that we can invite everyone we love to join us.

Communion is not just a distant hope; it's a reality that is already beginning to unfold. Each time we partake, we are reminded of God's faithfulness and the promise of provision that is as real now as it will be in the future. It's a taste of heaven, where the goodness is so pure and perfect that it can only be described as divine.

Yet Communion is more than just a personal experience; it's a powerful moment of community. It's a time when believers come together, united in our shared anticipation of what is to come. There is profound strength in this collective hope, in knowing that we are all awaiting the same incredible fulfillment.

So, what does this mean for our everyday life? It means that every time we take Communion, we are called to live with a sense of expectancy, much like preparing for a grand celebration. It's an invitation to ready our hearts and lives for the fullness of God's kingdom. Communion challenges us to live as though the feast has already begun—because, in many ways, it has. Every act of kindness, every pursuit of justice, every expression of love is a glimpse of what's to come.

Have you ever waited for a meal with great anticipation, knowing it would be deeply satisfying? Maybe, in preparation, you even broke into a happy dance. This should be our reaction to Communion, because it's not just a sacred tradition; it's a profound foretaste of the greatest feast ever—a feast that is still on the horizon, yet already breaking into our world. It's a moment to pause, to remember, and to kindle our excitement for the future that God has promised.

The Significance of Communion
1. A Memorial of Jesus's Sacrifice
In what ways does participating in Communion as a memorial of Jesus's sacrifice deepen my understanding of His love and forgiveness, and how can I carry this remembrance into my daily

life to foster a spirit of reconciliation and gratitude toward others?

___

Scriptural Reference:

- 1 Corinthians 11:24-25 (NIV): *"And when he had given thanks, he broke it and said, 'This is my body, which is for you; do this in remembrance of me.' In the same way, after supper he took the cup, saying, 'This cup is the new covenant in my blood; do this, whenever you drink it, in remembrance of me.'"*
- This passage emphasizes the importance of remembering Jesus's sacrifice through the act of communion.

2. A Symbol of Unity and Fellowship

In what ways does participating in Communion as a symbol of unity and fellowship encourage me to embrace and support fellow believers, and how can I actively work to foster love and reconciliation within my community, recognizing our interconnectedness as part of the body of Christ?

___

3. A Spiritual Nourishment

In what ways does participating in Communion as a source of spiritual nourishment deepen my relationship with Christ, the 'bread of life,' and how can I cultivate a greater dependence on God in my daily life?

_____

_____

_____

_____

4. A Foretaste of the Heavenly Feast
How does participating in Communion as a foretaste of the heavenly feast inspire me to live with hope and anticipation for the fulfillment of God's kingdom, and in what ways can I foster a spirit of celebration and unity within my community today?

_____

_____

_____

_____

Scriptural Reference:

- Revelation 19:9 (NIV): *"Then the angel said to me, 'Write this: Blessed are those who are invited to the wedding supper of the Lamb!' And he added, 'These are the true words of God.'"*
- This verse anticipates the ultimate celebration in God's kingdom, often envisioned as a grand feast.

The Connection to the Covenant of Provision
1. The Promise of Eternal Life
In what ways does the promise of eternal life, as symbolized in Communion, shape my understanding of God's commitment to fulfill His covenant, and how can I reflect this assurance in my daily life and spiritual journey?

_____

_____

_____

_____

The Table Book — Jermaine E. Pennington

2. A Reminder of God's Faithfulness

How does the practice of Communion serve as a reminder of God's faithfulness in providing for my physical and spiritual needs, and in what ways can I trust in His promise to sustain me through every aspect of my life?

_____

_____

_____

_____

_____

3. Encouraging a Life of Gratitude and Service

In what ways can I embody a life of gratitude and service inspired by Jesus's sacrificial love demonstrated in Communion, and how can I align my actions with the covenant's call for generosity, compassion, and the sharing of resources with others?

_____

_____

_____

_____

_____

4. A Call to Remember and Anticipate

How can I practice remembering Jesus's sacrifice through Communion while also cultivating a sense of anticipation for the fulfillment of God's promises, and in what ways can this perspective influence how I live my life in the present?

_____

_____

_____

_____

_____

Communion as a foretaste of the greater feast to come is a profound expression of the covenant of provision. It serves as a memorial of Jesus's sacrificial love, a symbol of unity among believers, and a source of spiritual nourishment. Through communion, believers are reminded of the promises of the new covenant, including the hope of eternal life and the assurance of God's ongoing provision. As a tangible reminder of these spiritual truths, communion encourages believers to live with gratitude, generosity, and a hopeful anticipation of the ultimate fulfillment of God's Kingdom. Let us approach the table with reverence and joy, recognizing communion as a sacred and transformative practice that connects us to the divine and to each other.

~The Passover Lamb is on the Menu~

We've entered into a family gathering, where there's one dish on the table that everyone is talking about. It's not just food; it's the centerpiece of the meal, the dish that ties everything together. In the story of faith, that dish is the Passover Lamb—a symbol so rich in meaning that it stands as the ultimate sign of deliverance and sacrifice in both Judaism and Christianity. This isn't just a tradition; it's the cornerstone of the covenant of provision, pointing directly to the sacrifice that sustains believers and secures their place at the eternal table.

In Jewish tradition, the Passover Lamb is central to the Exodus story. The scene: the Israelites are trapped in Egypt, enslaved and desperate for freedom. God's instructions are clear—each family must take a lamb, without blemish, and sacrifice it. They are to mark their doorposts with its blood, so the angel of death will pass over their homes. This act of faith and obedience marks the beginning of their journey to freedom, a journey that would define their identity as God's chosen people.

But the significance of the Passover Lamb doesn't end there. It becomes a lasting symbol of God's provision and deliverance, a reminder that even in the darkest times, hope remains. It's like that cherished family recipe, passed down through generations, reminding everyone of their roots and the strength that carried them through.

When we turn to the New Testament, the symbolism of the Passover Lamb takes on even greater depth in Christianity. Enter Jesus, the "Lamb of God." Just as the Passover Lamb was sacrificed to save the Israelites from physical death, Jesus' sacrifice is seen as delivering believers from spiritual death. If the Passover Lamb was the original recipe for deliverance, Jesus is the perfected version that fulfills and transcends it. His sacrifice on the cross isn't just a historical event; it secures a place at the eternal table for all who believe. This is the ultimate act of provision, ensuring that there is always enough grace, love, and forgiveness for everyone.

So, what does this mean for us today? The Passover Lamb is more than a historical symbol; it's a living testament to the covenant of provision that God extends to each of us. It's like knowing you have a reserved seat at the best table in the universe, where the menu is overflowing with grace, mercy, and eternal life.

This covenant of provision assures us that we're not just surviving—we're being sustained by the ultimate sacrifice. Just as the Israelites were provided for on their journey to the Promised Land, we are provided for on our journey through life. And this provision goes beyond just meeting our physical needs; it nourishes our souls, secures our place in God's family, and guarantees that we will never be left out of the eternal feast.

But understanding the symbolism of the Passover Lamb isn't just about basking in the benefits. It's also a call to action. Just as the lamb was sacrificed, we are called to live lives of sacrifice and service. It's about sharing the abundance we've received, inviting others to the table, and living in a way that reflects the love and sacrifice that have been extended to us.

This isn't about giving up everything we love; it's about living with purpose and focus on what truly matters. It's about being willing to give of ourselves—our time, our resources, our love—to ensure that others know they have a place at the table. It's about living in gratitude for the ultimate sacrifice that was made on our behalf and letting that gratitude inspire everything we do.

The Passover Lamb is more than an ancient tradition; it's a powerful reminder of a covenant that spans time and faith. It's a story of deliverance, sacrifice, and a love so profound that it ensures our place at the eternal table.

So, as we think of the Passover Lamb, remember that it's not just a symbol—it's a promise. A promise that we are provided for, that we are loved, and that we have a seat at the greatest feast ever prepared. And as we live out this promise, remember to invite others to the table, sharing the grace and provision that have been so generously given. Because in God's kingdom, there is always room for one more, and the feast is only just beginning.

The Historical and Religious Context

1. The Passover in Jewish Tradition

How can I appreciate the significance of the Passover in Jewish tradition and its connection to God's deliverance for the Israelites, and how might this understanding deepen my own faith and gratitude for the sacrifices made for my freedom?

_____
_____
_____
_____
_____

Scriptural Reference:

- Exodus 12:13 (NIV): *"The blood will be a sign for you on the houses where you are, and when I see the blood, I will pass over you. No destructive plague will touch you when I strike Egypt."*

- This passage highlights the role of the lamb's blood in protecting the Israelites and ensuring their deliverance.

2. The Passover Lamb in Christian Tradition

In what ways can I deepen my understanding of Jesus as the 'Lamb of God' and reflect on how His sacrifice provides me with deliverance from sin and death, and how can I share this profound truth with others?

_____
_____
_____
_____
_____

Scriptural Reference:

- John 1:29 (NIV): *"The next day John saw Jesus coming toward him and said, 'Look, the Lamb of God, who takes away the sin of the world!'"*
- This verse explicitly identifies Jesus as the Lamb of God, connecting the symbolism of the Passover Lamb to his role in the new covenant.

The Symbolism of the Passover Lamb

1. Symbol of Deliverance

How can I actively embrace the deliverance offered through the sacrifice of the Passover Lamb, both in my own life and in the lives of others, and what steps can I take to share the message of freedom and redemption with those around me?

_____
_____
_____
_____
_____

2. Symbol of Sacrifice

In what ways can I reflect on the significance of sacrifice in my own life, and how can I demonstrate love and self-giving in my relationships, inspired by the example of the Passover Lamb and Jesus's ultimate sacrifice?

_____
_____

3. Sustenance and Provision

In what ways do I recognize and appreciate the sustenance and provision that God offers me, both physically and spiritually, and how can I incorporate this understanding into my daily life and faith journey?

4. The Promise of the Eternal Table

How does the promise of the eternal table inspire me to live in anticipation of the heavenly banquet, and in what ways can I cultivate a spirit of celebration and gratitude for the victory over sin and death in my life today?

Scriptural Reference:

- Revelation 19:7-9 (NIV): *"Let us rejoice and be glad and give him glory! For the wedding of the Lamb has come, and his bride has made herself ready. Fine linen, bright and clean, was given her to wear. (Fine linen stands for the righteous acts of God's holy people.) Then the angel said to me, 'Write this: Blessed are those who are invited to the wedding supper of the Lamb!'"*

- This passage envisions the ultimate celebration in God's kingdom, where the Lamb's sacrifice is honored and all are welcome.

The Relevance to the Covenant of Provision

1. Assurance of Salvation and Security

In what ways does the symbolism of the Passover Lamb reassure me of my salvation and security in Christ, and how can I actively remind myself of the protection and promise that His sacrifice provides?

_____
_____
_____
_____
_____

2. Call to Remember and Celebrate

How can I actively remember and celebrate the sacrifice of the Passover Lamb in my life, and in what ways does participating in Communion deepen my understanding of Jesus's sacrifice and the covenant's promises?

_____
_____
_____
_____
_____

3. Embracing Sacrificial Love

In what ways can I embrace sacrificial love and service in my daily life, following the example of the Passover Lamb, and how can I reflect the covenant's values in my relationships and community?

_____
_____
_____

"The Passover Lamb is on the Menu" emphasizes the deep symbolism and significance of the Passover Lamb in the context of the covenant of provision. This symbol represents deliverance, sacrifice, sustenance, and the promise of eternal life. By understanding the Passover Lamb's role in both Jewish and Christian traditions, believers can appreciate the profound meaning of this imagery and its relevance to our faith. The covenant invites all to partake in the blessings and promises it offers, reminding believers of the ultimate provision and security found in the sacrifice of the Lamb. This sacred act embodies God's unwavering commitment to His people, drawing us into a covenant that fulfills every need. Let us remember and celebrate this profound act of love and embrace the call to live lives marked by sacrificial love, service, and unity in the spirit of the Lamb who provides. In embracing the Lamb, we find a place of unshakable belonging and peace, anchored in God's faithfulness. It is at this table of perpetual grace

~We Shall Never Hunger or Thirst Again~

As a child, I imagined adulthood as one grand adventure. Little did I know it's really just a daily, monotonous rerun of "What's for dinner?" The thought of never having to worry about meals, avoid that mid-afternoon slump, or fill some nagging sense of emptiness sounds almost too good to be true. And yet, the promise *"We Shall Never Hunger or Thirst Again"* is anything but a fairytale; it's the ultimate assurance woven into the covenant of provision—a promise of eternal satisfaction and fulfillment beyond our imagination. This isn't just about a future where our bellies are full and our cups overflow; it's about an all-encompassing contentment that meets every physical, spiritual, and emotional need.

Let's start with the essentials: food and drink. We all know the feeling of hunger or thirst—the empty stomach, the dry mouth, the relentless drive to satisfy those needs. But imagine a place where such feelings simply don't exist. Not because there's an endless supply of food and drink, but because we are completely, utterly, and eternally fulfilled.

In the Christian tradition, the phrase *"We Shall Never Hunger or Thirst Again"* offers a glimpse into the hope of eternal life—a life where every need, physical and beyond, is perfectly and perpetually met. It's like sitting at a banquet table that is always overflowing, where every dish is exquisitely satisfying, and there's never any fear of running out or being excluded. This is more than a metaphor; it's a profound promise that every longing, every desire will be fulfilled in the presence of the Provider.

But hunger and thirst are not confined to our physical bodies. We hunger for meaning, thirst for purpose, and long for connection. The promise of "never hungering or thirsting again" reaches into these deeper, more profound desires. It speaks of a state of existence where every spiritual and emotional need is met—where we are fully known, fully loved, and fully at peace.

Imagine a life where you never feel empty, never feel alone, never sense that something vital is missing. That's the heart of the covenant of provision. It's not just about having our physical needs met; it's about being so filled with love, joy, and purpose that there's nothing left to desire. It's like finding the final piece of the puzzle and realizing the picture is even more beautiful than you imagined.

This promise of never hungering or thirsting again is deeply embedded in Christian hope—the hope of eternal life with God. It's the belief in a future where all the brokenness of this world is healed, where every tear is wiped away, and where we are fully united with the One who provides for us in every way. It's the ultimate vision of abundance, where striving and searching are no longer necessary because everything we need is already ours.

But this promise isn't just a distant dream; it's a reality that believers can begin to experience here and now, in moments of divine provision and peace. It's like tasting that heavenly banquet in the midst of our daily lives—those moments when we feel truly content, truly at peace, and deeply connected to something greater than ourselves.

So how should we respond to this incredible promise? By embracing it with hope and expectation. We look forward to the day when we'll never hunger or thirst again, but we can also live in a way that reflects that promise today. This means trusting that God will provide for us—not just in the future, but in our everyday lives. It means seeking out the deeper satisfaction that comes from a relationship with the Provider, rather than chasing after temporary pleasures.

And here's the challenge: we're not just called to receive this promise; we're called to share it. As those who have tasted the goodness of God's provision, we are invited to bring a taste of that heavenly feast to others. Whether through acts of kindness, offering a listening ear, or sharing our resources with those in need, we can give others a glimpse of what it means to never hunger or thirst again.

"We Shall Never Hunger or Thirst Again" isn't just a future hope; it's a truth that can transform our lives right now. It's a reminder that we are provided for in every way, that we are loved beyond measure, and that our deepest needs will always be met. It's a call to live with hope, purpose, and the joy of knowing that we are on a journey toward a future where there is no lack, no longing, only perfect fulfillment.

So, the next time you feel that pang of hunger or thirst for something more, remember the promise that has been made to you. There's a seat at the table, a feast prepared, and a Provider who ensures that you will never be left wanting. Until that day comes, live in a way that reflects the abundance you've been promised—an abundance meant to be shared with the world. Because when we do that, we're not just waiting for the feast to come—we're already bringing a taste of it into the here and now.

The Promise of Eternal Satisfaction
1. Complete Fulfillment in the Presence of the Provider
How can I seek and cultivate a deeper awareness of the Provider's presence in my life, trusting that in Him I can find complete fulfillment—physically, spiritually, and emotionally—leading to a lasting sense of peace and contentment?

Scriptural Reference:

- Revelation 7:16-17 (NIV): *"Never again will they hunger; never again will they thirst. The sun will not beat down on them, nor any scorching heat. For the Lamb at the center of the throne will be their shepherd; 'he will lead them to springs of living water.' 'And God will wipe away every tear from their eyes.'"*
- This passage paints a vivid picture of the eternal satisfaction and protection promised to believers in the presence of God.

2. The Symbolism of Hunger and Thirst

In what ways can I acknowledge and bring my deep longings and needs to the Provider, trusting that my relationship with Him will fulfill both my physical necessities and the deeper desires of my soul?

3. The Role of the Provider

How can I more fully recognize and trust in the Provider's role in meeting not just my physical needs but also my spiritual and emotional needs, allowing His sustenance, care, and guidance to nurture every aspect of my life?

The Hope and Assurance of Eternal Provision

1. A Foretaste of Eternal Life

Considering the vast amount of manufactured lack that's fueled by greed, in what ways can I allow the promise of never hungering or thirsting again to sustain me through life's challenges and shape my sense of purpose and direction as I journey toward God's kingdom?

Scriptural Reference:

- John 6:35 (NIV): "Then Jesus declared, 'I am the bread of life. Whoever comes to me will never go hungry, and whoever believes in me will never be thirsty.'"
- Jesus's words affirm that he is the source of eternal life and satisfaction, offering spiritual nourishment that satisfies all who come to him.

2. The End of Suffering and Lack

In a mean cruel world that's full of trouble, tragedy, and trauma, how can I find comfort and strength in God's promise to end all suffering and lack, and live with hope and perseverance, knowing that my present struggles are only temporary?

3. The Invitation to All
In what ways can I embrace and reflect the inclusive nature of the covenant, sharing God's love and grace with others so that they, too, may experience the promise of eternal life?

_____
_____
_____
_____
_____

Reflections on Living in the Promise
1. Living with Hope and Gratitude
How can I cultivate a heart of hope and gratitude for God's eternal provision, allowing it to bring joy and peace into my daily life, even in challenging times?

_____
_____
_____
_____
_____

2. Embracing the Present with Faith
In what ways can I deepen my trust in God's provision today, allowing it to bring contentment and ease my worries about the future?

_____
_____
_____
_____
_____

3. Sharing the Promise with Others
How can I live out the covenant's promise of eternal provision through compassion and generosity, inviting others to experience God's hope and love?

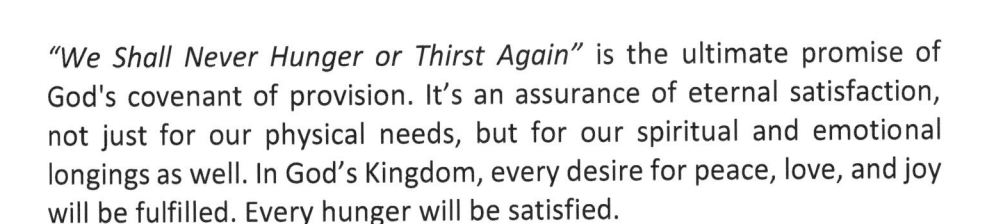

"We Shall Never Hunger or Thirst Again" is the ultimate promise of God's covenant of provision. It's an assurance of eternal satisfaction, not just for our physical needs, but for our spiritual and emotional longings as well. In God's Kingdom, every desire for peace, love, and joy will be fulfilled. Every hunger will be satisfied.

In a world that often feels like it's running on empty—where we face scarcity, hunger, thirst, and deep yearnings—this promise shines like a beacon of hope. Imagine a table prepared just for you in God's Kingdom, a table that overflows with abundance. No more worrying if there's enough, no more fear of going without. At this table, you're seen, loved, and fully provided for by the One who knows you best.

But here's the thing—this covenant of provision doesn't just point to the future. It's a call to live differently right now. It invites us to trust in God's care, to live with faith, gratitude, and to spread this hope to others. As we look forward to that eternal feast, we're also called to live like it's already happening. We're called to embrace the abundance we've been given and not hoard it, but instead, share it and make sure that everyone has a place at the table.

God's table isn't just a place where our needs get met. It's a place of grace and community, where we're reminded that we belong to something bigger than ourselves—a divine family, tied together by God's love and provision. As we gather at this table, we're nourished and transformed, empowered to share what we've received with others.

In this way, the covenant of provision is both a promise and a responsibility. It's the promise that we'll never hunger or thirst again in God's Kingdom, where every need is met with overflowing abundance.

But it's also the responsibility to live now in the light of that promise, to be sources of grace, love, provision for others and inclusion.

Take the story of Saint Damien of Molokai, for example. In the 19th century, this Belgian priest was sent to Hawaii to care for lepers on the island of Molokai. Leprosy was incurable, highly contagious, and those who had it were completely shunned. But Father Damien didn't shy away. One day, as a leper came to receive Holy Communion, Father Damien saw the man's severe condition—sores and all. Despite a moment of hesitation, he welcomed the man with open arms.

That act of inclusion was life-changing. The man, with tears in his eyes, whispered, *"Father, I've been excluded from receiving Holy Communion for so long. This is the first time I've felt worthy again."* Moved, Father Damien realized that Christ's love knows no boundaries—not disease, not stigma, nothing. From then on, he poured himself into ministering to these people, even at the cost of contracting the disease himself. In his suffering, he still celebrated Mass and shared the Eucharist with his flock, bringing them closer to Christ even as his own health failed.

Father Damien's life shows us the power of Holy Communion:

- Inclusion: He brought dignity and acceptance to the outcasts.
- Redemption: Christ's love went beyond physical suffering.
- Selflessness: His love for his people led him to risk his own life.

Just like Father Damien, the table of God's provision calls us to a deeper sense of community. As Desmond Tutu put it, *"The Eucharist reminds us that we are not alone, but part of a larger community."* As we reflect on this covenant, we hold tight to the promise of eternal satisfaction, but it also calls us to live with faith, gratitude, and generosity right now.

The table is set, the feast prepared, and there's a place for each of us. As we take our seat, let's remember to invite others—there's always room, enough to share, and a chance to spread God's hope and joy. By living this promise now, we not only look forward to God's Kingdom but bring a taste of it into today. May our lives reflect the abundant grace we've received, always drawing others to the table where *"We Shall Never Hunger or Thirst Again"* becomes reality.

Notes:

Chapter 1
1. 2. Corinthians 5:17, page 24
2. Colwin, Laurie, quote, page 26
3. Matthew 6:31-33, page 28
4. Psalm 23:1-3, page 29
5. Philippians 4:6-7, page 30
6. John 14:2-3, page 31

Chapter 2
7. Psalm 78:19-20, page 38
8. Matthew 7:9-11, page 40
9. Psalm 23:5, page 42
10. Acts 2:46, page 43
11. Psalm 104:14-15, page 47
12. John 6:35, page 47
13. Psalm 23:5-6, page 48
14. James 1:5, page 48
15. Philippians 4:19, page 49
16. Exodus 16:4, page 51
17. 1 Kings 17:14, page 51
18. Romans 14:2-3, page 54, 55
19. Leviticus 11:46-47, page 56
20. 1 Corinthians 6:19-20, page 61
21. Proverbs 25:16, page 64
22. Rogers, Adrian, quote, page 64
23. John 6:27-32, page 65
24. John 6:32, 33, page 65
25. Giglio, Louie, quote, page 66
26. Ferrazzi, Keith, page 72

Chapter 3
27. Matthew 6:11, page 83
28. 1 Thessalonians 5:18, page 85
29. Psalm 103:2, page 92
30. James 1:17, page 98

Chapter 4

31. Proverbs 23:20-21, page 109
32. 2 Corinthians 9:6-7, page 109, 110
33. Tibetan Proverb, page 112
34. 1 Corinthians 10:31, page 115
35. Proverbs 14:30, page 120
36. Philippians 4:11-12, page 121
37. Proverbs 12:27, page 127
38. Luke 3:11, page 129
39. Luke 16:10, page 133
40. Hardin, Brian, quote, page 137

Chapter 5

41. Carella, Mia, quote, page 143
42. Matthew 20:16, page 146
43. Luke 14:13-14, page 148
44. Luke 15:4-7, page 153
45. Luke 19:10, page 155
46. Matthew 25:40, page 160
47. Proverbs 31:8-9, page 162
48. Matthew 5:23-24, page 168, 169
49. Darwin, Charles, quote, page 177
50. Campbell, Caleb, quote, page 178
51. Matthew 21:13, page 180

Chapter 6

52. Luke 22:19-20, page 189
53. John 6:54, page 191
54. 1 Corinthians 11:24-25, page 195
55. Revelation 19:9, page 197
56. Exodus 12:13, page 201
57. John 1:29, page 202
58. Revelation 19:7-9, page 204
59. Revelation 7:16-17, page 208
60. John 6:35, page 210
61. Tutu, Desmond, page 213

Made in the USA
Columbia, SC
22 November 2024